We're heads!!!!

Illustrations by Devin Taylor
Design by Lindsay Broderick
Editorial by Erin Zimring

Copyright © 2020 ABC Studios

All rights reserved. Published by Kingswell, an imprint of Buena Vista Books, Inc.
No part of this book may be reproduced or transmitted in any form or by any means,
electronic or mechanical, including photocopying, recording, or by any information
storage and retrieval system, without written permission from the publisher.

All third-party trademarks and brands mentioned in this cookbook are property
of their respective owners. They are used for identification purposes only,
and do not imply endorsement.

For information address Kingswell, 1200 Grand Central Avenue,
Glendale, California 91201.

First Hardcover Edition, September 2020
1 3 5 7 9 10 8 6 4 2
ISBN 978-1-368-01068-9
Library of Congress Control Number: 2020937332
FAC-034274-20234

Printed in the United States of America

Visit www.disneybooks.com

The Golden Girls
COOKBOOK

MORE THAN 90 DELECTABLE RECIPES
FROM BLANCHE, ROSE, DOROTHY, AND SOPHIA

CHRISTOPHER STYLER

FOOD PHOTOGRAPHY BY ANDREW SCRIVANI

KINGSWELL

LOS ANGELES • NEW YORK

Recipes
Breakfast & Brunch

Soups & Salads

Veggie Sides

Pastas

Mains

Desserts

Party Foods & Drinks

Cheesecake!

Picture it: Miami, nineteen eighty-five . . .
Four women, friends. They laugh, they cry,
they eat. They love, they hate, they eat. Every
time you turn around, they eat.

Dorothy

Where are you going?

To either get ice cream or commit a felony. I'll decide in the car.

The thing we all know about Dorothy is that she's competent. It may not seem sexy, but her no-nonsense approach to life is actually a very attractive quality. Dorothy calls 'em like she sees 'em and uses her smarts to get results with minimal fuss. That's also the way she cooks.

Sure, Sophia knows all the treasured old-country recipes, but Dorothy's strong suits are in organization and cooking tasty meals using time-saving strategies. The reason we rarely see her cooking is because so many of her meals are prepped ahead or even made completely ahead of time. Take a look at the way Dorothy sets herself up for success in the Stir-Fried Shrimp, Snow Pea, and Walnut Salad or the breakfast-ready (Almost) Unsweetened Granola.

Being progressive, modern, and well-informed means Dorothy also keeps an eye on the healthfulness and quality of what she cooks. There are a lot of vegetable side dishes, salads, and light dishes, and even a refreshing citrus-based cocktail in the form of her Lemon-Basil Cooler.

Whether she's entertaining "the hunk from the center," Uncle Angelo, or even having Barbara Thorndyke over for coffee, Dorothy approaches it with a do-ahead mentality and a generous helping of self-confidence. We can all learn a lot from Dorothy.

(Almost) Unsweetened Granola

When the girls went as a group to visit a psychiatrist, it was revealed that Dorothy's organizational skills get on the other girls' nerves. Dorothy pays that no mind and continues to plan ahead for sensible workday meals.

MAKES: 3½ CUPS • PREP TIME: 5 MINUTES • COOK TIME: 30 MINUTES (MOSTLY UNATTENDED)

2 cups old-fashioned oats (not quick-cooking oats)

¾ cup coarsely chopped or slivered almonds

½ cup unsweetened flaked coconut (bigger flakes are better)

⅓ cup raw pepitas (pumpkin seeds)

3 tablespoons flax seeds, optional

1 tablespoon vegetable oil

1 tablespoon agave nectar or 1½ tablespoons maple syrup

1 teaspoon sesame oil

½ teaspoon pure vanilla extract

¼ teaspoon salt

¾ cup raisins or dried blueberries

1 Preheat the oven to 300°F.

2 Be smart (like Dorothy) and work clean: Measure out the oats, nuts, coconut, pepitas, and flax seed (if using) onto an 18 x 13-inch baking sheet. Whisk the vegetable oil, agave nectar, sesame oil, vanilla extract, and salt together in a large bowl. Add the oat mix and mix all ingredients—using your hands is easiest and you can "massage" the agave and oil into the dry ingredients—until well blended and the agave and oil are evenly distributed. Empty out the bowl onto the baking sheet and shake the pan to make an even layer. (There, you've only got three things to clean!)

3 Bake 15 minutes. Use a flat metal spatula to turn and stir the granola, mixing thoroughly so all the ingredients bake and brown evenly. Scatter the raisins or blueberries over the granola and turn and mix again. Continue baking, turning once more, until the oats and coconut are deep golden brown, about 15 minutes. Cool completely.

GOLDEN WISDOM

Avoid dried cranberries—they're almost always sweetened—for this recipe.
The idea is to keep added sugar low.

Measure the oil first; then the agave nectar will just slip out of the measuring spoon.

A note on the texture: This granola contains so little sugar and fat that it will not stick together and form clusters. The loose texture is perfect for sprinkling over yogurt, ice cream, salads, and side dishes where a little crunch is welcome, like mashed sweet potatoes.

Brooklyn Deli-Style Whitefish Salad

Dorothy loves Sophia's cooking, of course, but having grown up in Brooklyn, she misses a lot of the old neighborhood treats, like great Chinese takeout and hot dogs on the boardwalk at Coney Island. When Dorothy is feeling nostalgic for good Jewish deli, a nice bowl of whitefish salad does the trick. Look for vacuum-packed whitefish in the fish or deli departments of supermarkets.

MAKES: 1½ CUPS • PREP TIME: 20 MINUTES

1 medium celery stalk, trimmed and finely chopped (about ¼ cup)

3 tablespoons mayonnaise

1 medium scallion, trimmed and finely chopped (about 3 tablespoons)

2 tablespoons chopped fresh dill

1 tablespoon full-fat sour cream

¾ pound whitefish (with bones and skins)

A few grinds fresh black pepper

1 Mix the celery, mayonnaise, scallion, dill, and sour cream together in a medium bowl. Set aside.

2 Take a good look at the fish before you even touch it. You are going to be taking out all the bones, so it's helpful to know where they are before you go to work. (The skin is easy; you can't miss it!) Gently pull off the skin and run your finger or a spoon along the backbone to remove the very fatty meat, along with some bones. Starting at the backbone, gently pull the meat away from the bones in large pieces. Pull off the darker yellow-brown membrane along the belly side of the bones. Get rid of the skin and bones. Break the fish apart into smallish flakes, looking for and getting rid of any bones you come across in the process. Remove as many bones as you can. Pick out anything else that isn't the wonderful, moist meat of the fish.

3 Put the flakes in the bowl with the dressing. Toss gently—overmixing will turn this into the kind of whitefish salad mush that you find in so many delis. Last call: check for escapee bones as you gently mix! Taste for seasoning; it's unlikely you'll need salt, but several grinds of black pepper will definitely help. Serve the salad right away or refrigerate up to 3 days. Bring the salad to room temperature before serving.

Caesar a la Zbornak

This is not a traditional Caesar salad, but Dorothy is not a traditional woman. Why can't she have roasted red peppers and cherry tomatoes on her Caesar? Do YOU want to tell her no? And while Dorothy loves the creaminess of old-school Caesar dressing made with raw egg, she'd rather not make it that way, given Ma's advanced age. Mayonnaise gives her the same creaminess, and Ma never needs to know.

MAKES: 4 SERVINGS • PREP TIME: 20 MINUTES • COOK TIME (FOR CROUTONS, MOSTLY UNATTENDED): 20 MINUTES

DRESSING:

2 tablespoons mayonnaise

2 tablespoons lemon juice

3 cloves Roasted Garlic (page 22)

4 anchovy fillets

⅓ cup olive oil

¼ cup grated Parmesan cheese

Salt (if necessary) and freshly ground black pepper

SALAD:

Salad Croutons (page 159)

1 heart of romaine

A handful of baby arugula, optional

15 (or so) cherry tomatoes

½ cup roasted red pepper strips

3-4 (or more!) anchovy fillets, optional

1 grilled chicken breast, homemade (page 14) or store-bought, diced

Small block of Parmesan cheese, for shaving

DRESSING:

Blend the mayonnaise, lemon juice, roasted garlic cloves, and anchovies on low speed until very well blended. With the motor running, pour in the olive oil, stopping once or twice to scrape down the sides of the blender jar. Scrape the dressing into a small bowl and whisk in the Parmesan and salt (if necessary) and pepper to taste. Keep the dressing at room temperature for up to 3 hours or refrigerate for up to a day, bringing to room temperature before serving.

SALAD:

1 Make the croutons.

2 Trim any tired-looking outer leaves from the lettuce. Cut the head in half lengthwise and cut out the core. Cut the lettuce leaves into 1½-inch pieces. Add the arugula, if using, and wash and spin dry the greens.

3 Just before serving, line a large, wide salad bowl with the greens. Cut the cherry tomatoes in half. Scatter the tomatoes, red pepper strips, diced chicken, and anchovies (if using) over the greens. Drizzle half the dressing over the salad and, using a potato peeler, shave the Parmesan over all.

4 Bring the salad to the table, toss, and serve, passing the remaining dressing.

13

Dorothy's Guide to Packing a Workday Lunch

THE PLAN

Take about an hour to deposit delicious homemade food in your "bank" on Sunday. Withdraw from the bank for healthy ready-made lunches during the week. Here's a list of foods for stocking the bank. They are only suggestions, of course. If pita chips aren't your thing, substitute a few cucumber rounds instead.

PROTEINS

Quinoa: Measure ¾ cup quinoa into a sieve. Rinse under cool water for 2 to 3 minutes. Drain. Heat 1 cup water to boiling in a small saucepan. Add a big pinch of salt. Spoon the quinoa from the sieve into the saucepan (that's the easiest way to get it from point A to point B). When the water returns to a boil, cover the pan, put it over the lowest heat possible, and set a timer for 18 minutes. Remove the cover and check—the liquid should be completely absorbed. Refrigerate for up to 4 days.

Grilled Chicken Breast: Easy-peasy. Lay one or two chicken breasts out on a small baking pan. Drizzle one side with olive oil and season generously with salt and pepper. Flip and repeat. Let the chicken soak in the flavors for 1 to 2 hours in the refrigerator. Grill, panfry, or broil.

Hummus: Pack up some of Dorothy's Warm White Bean Hummus (page 22), but enjoy it cold. Or pick the supermarket hummus of your choice.

Hard-Boiled Eggs: Put as many eggs as you'd like to cook in a saucepan that fits them snugly. Pour in cold water to cover. Heat the water to a boil, then immediately adjust the heat so the water is at a bare simmer. Cook for 11 minutes. Cool eggs by placing them into an ice water bath for a few minutes.

Cheeses: Anything goes! If desk-dining on softer cheeses, like Brie or Camembert, take them out of the fridge about an hour before lunch time to give them time to warm up. But remember your officemates. Your love of Limburger may not extend to the next cubicle, but the aroma almost certainly will.

Beans: Choose firm beans, like chickpeas, black beans, or pigeon peas. Drain them, rinse them under cool water, and drain them again before packing them up.

LEFTOVERS

Salmon Fillet: Put another in the pan when you're making the recipe on page 32. Once cooked, it will remain fresh-tasting for 2 to 3 days.

Chicken: Remove the skin and shred the meat so it is easier to toss with other ingredients.

Vegetable: Whether it's the cauliflower on page 180, the carrots on page 123, or the dilled potatoes on page 83, any veg that you have conjured up for dinner the night before can be repurposed for lunch.

Rice: When making basic rice, always plan ahead and cook extra. Rice makes a nice bed for just about any mix of proteins and vegetables.

SALADS AND VEGETABLES

Greens: Select your favorites from among radicchio, romaine, Belgian endive, or red or green leaf lettuce. Cut them into bite-size pieces, then wash the greens and spin them dry. Most will hold for at least 3 days if you wrap them in paper towels after spinning, then tuck into a plastic bag. Don't tie or seal the bag. Endive and romaine may turn brown around the edges after a day or two, so plan to eat those early in the week.

Salad Staples:

• Peel carrots and grate them coarsely. Refrigerate in a small closed container.

• Cut thick-ish slices of cucumber and beets and store them as you would carrots.

• Steam cauliflower and broccoli florets (see Golden Cauliflower Trees, page 180, for info on how to cut them). Make sure to pat them dry before storing or they will develop an unpleasant smell after a couple of days.

SALAD ADD-ONS

Toasted Nuts: Toast nuts (hulled sunflower seeds and pepitas, too) on a baking pan in a 350°F oven until toasted all the way through. Shake the pan a few times during toasting so the nuts toast evenly. General times: about 16 minutes for whole, dense nuts like almonds and hazelnuts; 13 minutes for softer whole nuts like pecans and walnuts; 9 to 10 minutes for pepitas, sliced or slivered almonds, or sunflower seeds.

Pita Chips: Pull pocket-style pita bread into two rounds by working a finger or paring knife around the edges. Cut the rounds into wedges, 8 for large pitas or 6 for small pitas. Toast in a 350°F oven, stirring and flipping once, until crisp and lightly toasted, about 15 minutes.

Salad Croutons (page 159)

Toasted Tortilla Strips: Cut corn tortillas into thin strips. Spread the strips out on a baking sheet and toast in a 350°F oven, stirring once, until lightly browned, about 10 minutes.

DRESSINGS

Sneak some of Blanche's 1-2-3 Citrus Dressing (page 119) or Avocado-Dill-Yogurt Dressing (page 117) when she's not looking. Or make a simple vinaigrette by whisking together 3 parts olive oil (or other oil of your choice), 1 part vinegar, and a dab of mustard. Season with salt and pepper. Be sure to store the dressing in a container with a tight-fitting lid so you can shake it up at work. Empty spice bottles with lids are perfect for this.

PANTRY/FREEZER/FRIDGE STAPLES

Dried blueberries or cranberries
Whole-grain wraps
Rice cakes
Frozen rice or quinoa (which you cleverly hid in the freezer last time you cooked some)
Tuna (packed how you like it)
Seasoned popcorn (your own or store-bought)

OTHER LUNCH CHOICES

1 portion Roasted and Mashed Sweet Potatoes (page 38), sprinkled
with lots of toasted slivered almonds
Brooklyn Deli–Style Whitefish Salad (page 12)
Simplest Lemon-Herb Chicken (page 24)
Chunky Minestrone (page 151)
Lindstrom Surprise (page 72)

WHAT TO DO WITH ALL THIS?

MONDAY
Mixed greens
Spice jar of shakable dressing
Shredded chicken
Two or three vegetables for mixing
Toss them together, and voilà!

TUESDAY
Hummus
Pita chips and/or cucumber rounds for dipping
Chip-and-dip it!

WEDNESDAY
Roasted beets
Spice jar of shakable dressing
Flaked salmon
Toasted pepitas
Toss the beets and dressing, plate side-by-side with the salmon, and scatter pepitas on top.

THURSDAY
It's clean out the fridge day—you know there are lots of good things in there.

FRIDAY
Leave work early, go to happy hour at Julio's, and dine on peanuts from the bar.

— OR —

MONDAY
Quinoa
Spice jar of shakable dressing
Shredded carrots, toasted slivered almonds, steamed broccoli
Toss them together and enjoy!

TUESDAY
Rice cake
Shredded chicken
Grated jack or cheddar cheese
Spicy bottled salsa
Top rice cakes with shredded chicken and grated cheese. Microwave just long enough to melt cheese. Top with salsa. There you have it: under a minute to Tostadas de la Microwave!

WEDNESDAY
That fridge is looking like it needs cleaning again!

THURSDAY
Tuna
String beans
Hard-boiled eggs
Potatoes
Cherry tomatoes
Simple vinaigrette
Arrange your own salade Niçoise.

FRIDAY
Leave work early; take Ma for shoes at Shimshack's.

Fennel, Orange, and Feta Salad

The perfect salad for winter, when oranges and fennel are at their best. Perfect with pan-grilled or broiled salmon or chicken.

MAKES: 4 TO 6 SERVINGS • PREP TIME: 15 MINUTES

1 medium head fennel

2 large Cara Cara or navel oranges

¼ pound feta, crumbled (about 1 cup)

½ small red onion, sliced very thin

3 tablespoons olive oil

Coarse sea salt (Maldon is ideal here) or kosher salt

1 Pull enough fronds from the fennel stalks to measure ½ cup very loosely packed. Cut the stalks flush with the top of the bulb and discard them. Turn the bulb upside down and cut in quarters through the core. Cut out the pieces of core and slice the fennel as thin as you can. Put the fennel in a wide, shallow bowl.

2 Cut the oranges in half. Squeeze the juice of one half over the fennel. Place the other halves flat side down on a cutting board. With a small, sharp knife, cut away the peel and white pith, leaving as much of the rest of the orange intact as possible. Cut the peeled oranges into 1-inch pieces, flicking out seeds as you go. Add the orange to the bowl with the fennel.

3 Toss the fennel, oranges, and orange juice and make a layer of the fennel and oranges in the bowl. Make a well in the center and add the feta to the well. Scatter the onion slices over the fennel and oranges.

4 Drizzle the olive oil over the salad and bring to the table. Season with coarse salt and pepper and toss. Spoon onto serving plates.

Warm White Bean Hummus with Pita Wedges

MAKES: 4 SERVINGS • PREP TIME: 1 HOUR 20 MINUTES • WARM TIME: 10 TO 15 MINUTES

¼ cup olive oil

3 to 4 cloves Roasted Garlic (see below)

1½ teaspoons chopped fresh thyme leaves or ½ teaspoon dried thyme

One 15-ounce can white beans or 1½ cups cooked white beans

1 tablespoon tahini

2 tablespoons fresh lemon juice

Salt, for seasoning

Toasted sesame seeds (see "Everything" Mango-Pineapple Salad, page 100)

Whole-wheat pita wedges

1 Combine the olive oil, roasted garlic, and thyme in a small skillet. Heat over low heat until the thyme is sizzling. Remove and cool.

2 Give the beans, tahini, lemon juice, and olive oil mixture a whir in the blender or food processor until very smooth. Season with salt. Spoon the hummus into a 2-cup ramekin or baking dish. Sprinkle the toasted sesame seeds over the top and let stand at room temperature for up to 4 hours or refrigerate overnight. The hummus will be better if left to stand instead of being baked straightaway.

3 Heat the oven to 250°F. Warm the hummus for 10 to 15 minutes just before serving. Put the pita wedges in the oven during the last 5 minutes of heating. Serve the dip warm, letting people tear off pieces of the warm pita to use as dippers. Please don't microwave; Dorothy will never forgive you. She's like that.

ROASTED GARLIC

Slow cooking completely changes garlic: the cloves become butter-soft, deep golden brown, and sweet. Roasted garlic is wonderful in dips or for spreading right on Crostini (page 159). To prepare, use a serrated knife to cut off the tips of as many heads of garlic as you'd like to roast. You should be able to see the very tips of most if not all the garlic cloves inside. Gently peel away most of the papery cover, leaving the head of garlic intact. Shave off enough of the root end to help the head stand upright. Put the head(s) in a small baking dish. Drizzle them with olive oil and sprinkle them with salt. Cover the dish with aluminum foil and bake in a preheated 300°F oven until the cloves are tender, 45 minutes to an hour. Uncover and bake another 15 minutes to lightly brown the garlic. Remove from the oven and cool. Separate the cloves and squeeze the soft pulp from the cloves into a small glass dish. (Wear disposable gloves if you like.) Tamp down the garlic puree and cover it with a thin layer of olive oil. Cover the dish tightly with plastic wrap. The roasted garlic will keep in the refrigerator for up to a week.

Jazzed-Up Turkey Meat Loaf

A dish Dorothy prepared for her son, Michael, a jazz musician, on one of his visits.

MAKES: 4 SERVINGS • PREP TIME: 15 MINUTES • COOK AND REST TIME: 55 MINUTES (UNSUPERVISED)

2 tablespoons vegetable oil

1 small red or yellow onion, finely diced (about 1 cup)

1 medium carrot, peeled and coarsely shredded

2 cloves garlic, minced

1 egg

1 tablespoon tamari soy sauce

1 tablespoon Worcestershire or hoisin sauce

1 tablespoon Dijon mustard

1 pound ground turkey

⅓ cup quick-cooking oats

2 tablespoons tomato paste

2 tablespoons panko bread crumbs, for coating

1 Preheat the oven to 400°F with a rack in the center position.

2 Heat the oil in a small skillet over medium heat. Add the onion, carrot, and garlic and cook, stirring frequently, until the onion is softened, about 4 minutes. Scrape the vegetables into a large bowl and cool to room temperature.

3 Add egg, soy sauce, Worcestershire, and mustard to the bowl. Beat with a fork until very well blended. Crumble the turkey into the bowl, scatter the oats over the turkey, and mix everything together very well. Put the meat loaf mixture onto a baking sheet and shape into a loaf about 8 inches long by 4 inches wide.

4 Brush the tomato paste over the top and sides of the meat loaf. Scatter the panko over the tomato paste.

5 Bake until the outside is well browned and the turkey is cooked through, about 45 minutes. An easy way to tell if the center is cooked is to stick a paring knife into the thickest part of the loaf. The juices that run out will be clear and not pink if the loaf is fully cooked. Let the turkey loaf stand 10 minutes before cutting.

GOLDEN WISDOM

This amount of oats will make a slightly loose-textured but moist meat loaf. For a firmer meat loaf, increase the amount of oats to ½ cup.

Simplest Lemon-Herb Chicken (Broiled, Sautéed, Grilled, or Roasted)

Dorothy's pragmatic side comes out in this incredibly simple main course that can be grilled, sautéed, roasted, or broiled. If you choose the grilled option, just hope a man dressed as a giant bird doesn't drop onto your lanai while you're at the grill.

MAKES: 4 SERVINGS • PREP TIME: 10 MINUTES • COOK TIME: ABOUT 20 MINUTES

2 lemons

¼ cup chopped mixed herbs, including any or all of the following: rosemary, sage, thyme, summer savory, tarragon, garlic chives

2 cloves garlic

1 teaspoon salt

Large pinch crushed red pepper

4 large (about 6-ounce) boneless/skinless chicken thighs

Olive oil

1 Squeeze the lemon juice into a medium bowl. Add the herbs, garlic, salt, and red pepper. Trim any excess fat from the chicken thighs and add them to the bowl. Toss around so all the chicken is coated.

2 Put the chicken and marinade into a 1-quart Ziploc bag. Squish the chicken around to coat all the pieces with the marinade. Refrigerate for 1 to 2 days, taking the bag out every once in a while and squishing the chicken around to make sure the pieces are marinating evenly.

3 When you're ready to cook the chicken, drain it thoroughly. Pour a little olive oil onto a plate and turn the chicken in the oil to lightly coat it.

4 However you cook the chicken, an instant-read thermometer is the way to go to determine doneness (page 29).

ROAST

Heat the oven to 500°F. Line a small baking sheet with aluminum foil and lightly oil the foil. Roast until the thighs are browned and cooked through, about 14 minutes.

BROIL

Set the oven rack about 8 inches from the heat source. Preheat the broiler (to high, if you have that option). Broil the chicken, turning only once, until it is well browned on at least one side and cooked through, about 10 minutes.

SAUTÉ

A nonstick pan works well. Heat the pan over medium-high heat. Cook the chicken until browned on both sides and cooked through, about 12 minutes. Adjust the heat so the chicken is not splattering wildly or just sitting there, but giving off a lively sizzle.

GRILL

Start a charcoal fire or preheat a gas grill to medium-high. In either case, the grill is ready when it passes the 4-second test—you can hold your palm about 6 inches above the grate for only 4 seconds before you need to pull it away. (As Dorothy might say: "Ma, give me a hand for a minute.") Lay the chicken onto the grill. Cook, turning only once, until the chicken is well browned and no trace of pink remains in the thickest part of the thigh. This will take about 10 to 12 minutes, depending on your grill. Two basic grilling tips: make sure your grill is good and clean (wire-brush clean), and use a paper towel dipped in vegetable oil and a pair of long tongs to oil the grill just before you put the chicken on it. Once the chicken is on the grill, resist the urge to flip it, move it, poke it, or do anything else for several minutes. If you let it just sit, it will free itself from the grill easily.

Chicken Piccata

Sophia never met a classic Italian menu item that she didn't think she could re-create. She handed that confidence down to Dorothy, along with a file box full of recipes, like this one for chicken brightly seasoned with capers and lemon juice.

MAKES: 4 SERVINGS • PREP TIME: 20 MINUTES • COOK TIME: 20 MINUTES

1/2 cup dry white wine

1 cup reduced-sodium chicken broth

2 tablespoons drained small (aka nonpareil) capers

3 tablespoons finely chopped Italian parsley

4 teaspoons fresh lemon juice (more or less to taste)

1¼ pounds "thin-sliced" boneless chicken breasts

Fine sea or kosher salt and freshly ground black pepper

All-purpose flour

2 tablespoons vegetable oil, or as needed

2 tablespoons butter, or as needed

1 Line up the measured wine, broth, capers, parsley, and lemon juice off to the side of the stove. Pat the chicken dry with paper towels and season both sides of each piece with salt and pepper. Lay a plate of the flour and an empty baking sheet next to the stove.

2 In a large, heavy sauté pan, heat oil and 1 tablespoon butter on medium until the butter is foaming. Working quickly, coat half the seasoned chicken with flour. Shake off excess flour and carefully lay the pieces into the pan in a single layer. Cook until undersides are lightly browned, then turn the pieces over. When the other sides are browned and the chicken feels firm to the touch, remove the chicken to the baking sheet. Repeat with the rest of the chicken. If necessary, add a bit more oil and butter to the pan.

3 When all the chicken is done, pour off any fat from the pan and return the pan to the heat. Give it a few seconds to heat back up and pour in the white wine. It should come to a boil almost immediately; cook, scraping the bottom of the pan, until the wine is almost completely evaporated. Pour in the stock and heat to a boil. Slip the chicken pieces into the stock and turn them in the liquid to heat them. There should be just enough stock to barely cover the chicken.

4 Add the parsley, capers, lemon juice, and remaining 1 tablespoon butter to the pan. Adjust the heat so the sauce is at a lively simmer. Continue turning the chicken in the sauce to coat the chicken and mix the parsley and capers throughout. When the sauce is lightly thickened, remove the pan from the heat and transfer the chicken to plates (or serve it Golden Girls style, on a platter) and spoon the sauce over it.

GOLDEN WISDOM

You can work with a pair of tongs to coat the chicken and lay it into the pan.

Dry-Rubbed Pork Tenderloin with Crunchy Salad

This dish serves four Golden Girls, including one octogenarian and one serial dieter; for heartier appetites, or if you like leftovers, prepare two tenderloins.

MAKES: 4 SERVINGS • PREP TIME: 10 MINUTES • COOK TIME: ABOUT 25 MINUTES

FOR THE DRY RUB:
(makes enough for 2 tenderloins):
¾ teaspoon ground coriander seed

½ teaspoon ground cumin seed

½ teaspoon smoked or regular sweet paprika

¼ teaspoon ground cinnamon

1 teaspoon sea salt

FOR THE SALAD:
3 tablespoons orange juice, fresh-squeezed or good-quality bottled

3 tablespoons vegetable oil

1 tablespoon honey or agave nectar

1 teaspoon Dijon mustard

¼ teaspoon salt

A few grinds black pepper

8 lightly packed cups trimmed and washed crunchy greens, "dealer's choice" (see notes)

MAKE THE DRY RUB/SEASON THE PORK:
1 Up to a day in advance: Combine all the dry rub ingredients and rub the pork with half the mix if preparing one tenderloin or all the mix if making two. Really rub the mix into the pork for the best flavor. Reserve extra dry rub for rubbing another pork tenderloin, hamburgers, steak, chicken, etc.

PREP THE SALAD:
2 Make the dressing: Combine the orange juice, vegetable oil, honey, mustard, salt, and pepper in a jar with a tight-fitting lid. Shake well and set aside. The dressing can be made up to the day before. Refrigerate in the jar, bring to room temperature, and shake well before using.

3 Trim the greens and cut into bite-size pieces. Wash well and spin in a salad spinner. Just before starting the pork, put the greens in a large bowl.

COOK THE PORK:
4 Rub the pork with just enough olive oil to make it glisten. Cook on a hot charcoal or gas grill, turning occasionally, until the thickest part of the tenderloin reaches 150°F on an instant-read thermometer. (See sidebar.) This will produce pork that is very slightly pink at the thickest part of the tenderloin and more well-done in thinner parts, so there's something for everyone. Remove the pork and let rest about 10 minutes.

FOR THE PORK:

One pork tenderloin, about 1½ pounds (see notes)

Olive oil to rub the pork

PLATE IT:

5 While the pork is resting, shake the dressing and pour it over the greens. Toss to mix. Arrange the salad on individual plates or a large platter if you'd like to serve the meal family style. Let the extra dressing run onto the plate or platter to season the slices of pork. Carve the pork into ½-inch-thick slices crosswise (against the grain) and arrange them on the plates or platter.

> It took me three and a half days to have Dorothy. I finally coaxed her out with a pork chop.

WHEN A MEAT THERMOMETER IS YOUR BEST FRIEND ————

Instant-read thermometers are the only way to be sure that the meat or poultry you are cooking has reached a safe temperature. Instant-read thermometers have come a long way. You should spend a few more dollars for a good-quality digital version, like those made by Thermapen. Always insert the tip of the thermometer into the thickest part of whatever you are cooking, and always away from the bone (which in many cases—like with roast chicken—will be cooler than the meat). Test the temperature in a few places to ensure all parts have reached the temperature indicated.

Notes: It can be difficult to find pork tenderloins that have not been vacuum-packed in brine. Avoid those whenever you can. The brine plumps up the meat with water and you may not like the flavor the brine imparts. (Plus, you don't know what's in that brine!) Look for loosely packed, "dry" pork tenderloin.

If you like to pick, trim, and wash your own blend of salad greens, go right ahead. Keep them crunchy—Little Gem, romaine, and Belgian endive, for example. If not, choose packaged salad greens with a variety of textures, such as equal parts Caesar salad mix and baby arugula.

If you don't own a salad spinner, get out your bus pass, go to a kitchenwares store, and pick one up. It's an indispensable piece of kitchen gear.

Stir-Fried Shrimp, Snow Pea, and Walnut Salad

Having all your ingredients prepped and set out, ready to roll, appeals to Dorothy's organizational skills. As she once said, "Since when is competence a crime?"

MAKES: 6 FIRST-COURSE OR 3 MAIN-COURSE SERVINGS • PREP TIME: 20 MINUTES • COOK TIME: 20 MINUTES ——

10 cups whole small lettuce leaves, about 20 leaves, torn into big pieces (radicchio, Belgian endive, Bibb and/or romaine hearts)

½ cup 1-2-3 Citrus Dressing (page 119)

1 tablespoon peanut or canola oil

¾ cup walnut halves or pieces

¾ pound medium (about 25 per pound) shrimp, shelled (including tails) and deveined

¼ pound snow peas

Coarse sea salt, such as Maldon or other "finishing" salt

DRESS-UPS (none, any, or all):
Cherry tomatoes, halved

Cucumber chunks

Avocado, peeled, pitted, and diced

1   In advance: Wash and spin or drain the salad greens. Make the dressing. Set out everything you need and ask Ma to help you set the table just before you get started.

2   Line a large salad bowl with the lettuce leaves, leaving space in the center of the bowl.

3   Heat the peanut or canola oil in a large (12-inch) skillet over medium heat. Add the walnuts. Sauté, tossing occasionally, until lightly browned, about 3 minutes. Add the shrimp and toss them around until cooked through, about 4 minutes. Add the snow peas and toss just until they turn bright green—a matter of seconds. Remove the pan from the heat.

4   Drizzle 3 tablespoons of the dressing over the lettuce leaves. Pour another 2 to 3 tablespoons over the shrimp and snow peas in the pan and toss them to coat with the dressing, scraping up the goodness that is stuck to the bottom of the pan as you go. Turn the stir-fried shrimp into the center of the bowl. Make a ring around the shrimp/snow peas of whichever dress-ups you are using. Bring the salad to the table and sprinkle lightly with the salt. Toss together before serving. Pass any remaining dressing around separately, if you like. For less of a production, toss all ingredients and make individual plates to serve.

Crunchy Mustard-Dill Salmon

Perfect for one of Dorothy's date nights at home. Maybe with Frank, "the hunk from the center"?

MAKES: 2 SERVINGS • PREP TIME: 15 MINUTES • COOK TIME: 12 TO 15 MINUTES

Vegetable oil or nonstick cooking spray

Two 6- to 8-ounce salmon fillets

Coarse sea or kosher salt

Freshly ground black pepper

3 tablespoons chopped fresh dill or 1 teaspoon dried tarragon

2 teaspoons olive oil

2 teaspoons Dijon mustard

1 teaspoon lemon juice

½ cup Toasted Panko (see below)

1 Line a small baking sheet with aluminum foil. Brush the foil with vegetable oil or spray with nonstick vegetable cooking spray. Pat the salmon fillets dry with paper towels. Season the fillets with salt and pepper, rubbing the seasoning into the meat, and place the fillets on the prepared baking sheet skin side down. Stir the dill, olive oil, mustard, and lemon juice together in a small bowl until blended. Brush the top and sides of the salmon with the mustard-dill mix. Refrigerate for at least 30 minutes and up to 3 hours.

2 Heat the oven to 450°F with a rack in the center position. Place the tray of salmon toward the back of the oven (usually the hottest place in the oven) and bake to your desired doneness.

3 Remove and cool for a minute or two. Sprinkle the toasted panko over the sauce that coats the top and sides of the fillets to cover it more or less completely with golden deliciousness and crunch. Serve immediately.

GOLDEN WISDOM

Think of Toasted Panko as a condiment—a very cheap, easy-to-make condiment. Sprinkle it over soups, simple pasta dishes, sautéed vegetables, and more. To make, spread out 1 cup panko on a baking sheet and bake in a 350°F oven until golden brown, stopping to stir once, about 5 minutes. Remove and cool. Store in an airtight container at room temperature for up to 3 weeks.

For Whom the Stuffed Bell Pepper Tolls

Dorothy may have made a bad choice when she ignored her best friends Rose and Blanche to spend time with snooty author Barbara Thorndyke. But she didn't make the wrong choice at lunch when she ordered this hearty bell pepper filled with beef, rice, and tomato. You can also substitute a vegetarian filling featuring kale and black beans.

MAKES: 4 STUFFED PEPPERS • PREP TIME: 30 MINUTES • COOK TIME: 50 MINUTES (UNATTENDED)

FOR THE FILLING:

1 pound lean (90% lean) ground beef

1 medium yellow onion, diced (about 1 cup)

2 medium carrots, coarsely shredded (about ¾ cup)

1½ cups cooked rice

One 8-ounce can or 1 cup tomato sauce

½ teaspoon dried oregano

Fine sea or kosher salt and freshly ground black pepper

1 cup shredded Muenster or Monterey Jack cheese

TO FILL AND BAKE THE PEPPERS:
4 medium to large yellow or red bell peppers, wider than they are tall (about 1¾ pounds)

½ cup Rotisserie Chicken Broth (page 71) or store-bought reduced-sodium chicken broth

¼ cup tomato sauce

MAKE THE FILLING:

1 Crumble the ground beef into a large deep skillet over medium heat. Cook the beef a few minutes, stirring, until the liquid is evaporated and the beef begins to sizzle. If there is more than a tablespoon or so of fat left in the pan, tilt the pan and carefully spoon out and discard the excess fat, leaving 1 tablespoon behind.

2 Stir in the onion and carrot and cook until the carrot is tender, about 3 minutes. Add the rice, tomato sauce, and oregano and heat to a boil. Remove from the heat. Season to taste with salt and pepper. Let cool to room temperature, then stir in the cheese.

FILL AND BAKE THE PEPPERS:

3 Heat the oven to 375°F with a rack in the center position.

4 Mix the chicken broth and ¼ cup tomato sauce in an 8-inch square baking dish or other dish in which the peppers fit snugly. Shave a very thin layer off the bottom of the peppers—just enough to help the peppers stand upright; don't cut into the inside of the pepper. Cut the top ½ inch off the peppers. Scrape seeds and ribs from the inside and top of each pepper. Trim the stem to look nice. Fill the peppers, packing the filling very lightly, level with the top of the peppers. (You may have a little filling left over.) Fit the tops back on and cover the baking dish tightly with aluminum foil.

5 Bake until the peppers are tender and the filling is heated through, 50 minutes to 1 hour. Let stand 10 to 15 minutes. Carefully lift the peppers onto plates. Lift up the top, drizzle some of the baking juices over the filling, and close the peppers back up.

Vegetarian Tex-Mex Filling (Alternate Filling)

PREP TIME: 15 MINUTES • COOK TIME: 20 MINUTES

1 tablespoon vegetable oil

1 large yellow onion, diced (about 1½ cups)

2 medium carrots, coarsely shredded (about ¾ cup)

4 cups stemmed and thinly sliced kale (about 4 ounces)

One 8-ounce can (or 1 cup) tomato sauce

One 15-ounce can black beans, drained and rinsed

¾ cup roasted corn kernels (page 174), frozen corn kernels, or frozen baby peas

½ teaspoon ground coriander

¼ teaspoon ground cumin

Fine sea or kosher salt and freshly ground black pepper

¾ cup shredded pepper jack cheese

1 Heat the vegetable oil in a large deep skillet over medium heat. Stir in the onion and carrot and cook until the carrot is tender, about 3 minutes. Stir in the kale and cook, stirring, until wilted but still bright green, about 5 minutes. Stir in the tomato sauce, black beans, corn, coriander, and cumin. Heat to boiling and season with salt and pepper. Remove from heat and let cool to room temperature before stirring in the cheese. Fill, bake, and serve as above.

I've never seen a menu with a table of contents before!

Skip ahead to chapter five. It's the lunch menu.

Barbara Thorndyke

Baked Chickpea and Kale Casserole

Dorothy's Italian roots are on display with this blend of chickpeas, sun-dried tomatoes, bitter greens, and olive oil. A little side trip across the Mediterranean to Greece for the feta rounds out this very simple dish.

MAKES: 4 SERVINGS • PREP TIME: 25 MINUTES • COOK TIME: 25 MINUTES (MOSTLY UNATTENDED)

¾ pound kale, preferably Lacinato kale

¼ cup panko breadcrumbs

1 tablespoon olive oil

Two 15-ounce cans low-sodium chickpeas, drained and rinsed

¼ cup bottled chopped sun-dried tomatoes in olive oil, plus 2 tablespoons of the oil from the jar

½ cup chicken broth

4 large scallions, trimmed and thinly sliced

3 ounces feta cheese, crumbled (about ¾ cup)

¼ teaspoon salt

1 Trim and rinse kale as described for the collards in the recipe for Naughty Blanche Collard Greens (page 125). Cut the rinsed kale into very thin strips. There will be about 4 lightly packed cups. Rub the panko and olive oil together in a small bowl with your fingertips until well blended and set aside.

2 Preheat the oven to 400°F with a rack in the center position.

3 Put half the drained and rinsed chickpeas in a medium bowl. Add the sun-dried tomatoes and their oil. Mash with an old-school potato masher (Sophia has one in her suitcase) or a large slotted spoon until the chickpeas are finely mashed. Stir in the chicken broth, then the remaining chickpeas, shredded kale, scallion, feta, and salt. Let stand about 10 minutes, until the kale wilts a little.

4 Scrape the mixture into an 8 x 8-inch baking dish. Cover with aluminum foil and bake 20 minutes. Remove the foil and scatter the oiled breadcrumbs in an even layer over the top. Bake until the edges of the casserole are bubbling and the panko topping is golden brown, 15 to 20 minutes. Let stand 10 to 15 minutes before serving. Serve hot or warm.

Notes: Turn leftovers of this casserole into chickpea pancakes! First, check the seasoning of the leftovers; chilling and reheating can dull the flavors. For every 1½ cups, beat in 1 egg. If you have more or less than 1½ cups, don't worry. Your finished pancakes will be either a little moister or a little drier and crumblier. Form into medium-sized pancakes (about ½ cup per pancake). Pour a little olive oil into a large, heavy sauté pan or onto a griddle and heat. Slip the pancakes into the pan and cook, turning once, until lightly browned on both sides and warmed through, about 5 minutes.

Alternately, you can warm the leftovers and stir them into a potful of brown or white rice for a super-simple side dish or main course.

The casserole may be prepared 2 hours ahead and kept at room temperature or up to 2 days in advance and refrigerated. But if making ahead, rub the panko and olive oil together just before baking.

Roasted and Mashed Sweet Potatoes

Dorothy, being the most pragmatic of the Golden Girls in all matters, including culinary, doesn't see the purpose of piling more sweet ingredients into a recipe for sweet potatoes. She picks just a few ingredients—tangy sour cream, fresh chives, and toasted pecans—that complement the natural sweetness of the sweet potatoes.

MAKES: 3½ CUPS • PREP TIME: 5 MINUTES • COOK TIME: 1½ HOURS (MOSTLY UNATTENDED) ————

3 sweet potatoes (about 1½ pounds)

⅓ cup sour cream

3 tablespoons butter

½ teaspoon fine sea or kosher salt, or more to taste

Several grinds of black pepper

¼ cup toasted chopped pecans

2 tablespoons thinly sliced chives or ½ cup sliced scallion greens

1 Heat the oven to 425°F.

2 Scrub the sweet potatoes and dry them well. Put the sweet potatoes right on the oven rack, with a sheet of aluminum foil on the rack below, and roast until the skin is well browned and you can poke right through to the center easily with a paring knife, 45 minutes to an hour, depending on size. Remove and cool the sweet potatoes just long enough to be able to handle them.

3 Split the sweet potatoes lengthwise and scoop out the pulp into a bowl, using a towel or pot holder to protect your hand. (If your sweets allow it, simply pull off the skins.) Beat in the sour cream, butter, salt, and pepper. Transfer to an 8 x 5-inch baking dish or 4-cup soufflé dish. The finished sweet potatoes may be kept at room temperature for up to 4 hours.

4 To serve, preheat oven to 375°F. Bake uncovered for 30 minutes. Scatter toasted pecans and chives over the top.

Stir-Fried Broccoli Slaw Salad

This is a perfect side dish for just about anything, from hamburgers to salmon. It is best when made ahead so you can get it out of the way hours before mealtime!

MAKES: 6 SERVINGS • PREP TIME: 10 MINUTES • COOK TIME: 5 MINUTES

2 tablespoons mayonnaise

1 tablespoon white wine vinegar or lemon juice

1½ teaspoons sugar

3 scallions

2 tablespoons vegetable oil

1 tablespoon finely chopped ginger

2 cloves garlic, finely chopped

One 12-ounce bag broccoli slaw mix

Fine sea salt

1 Stir the mayonnaise, vinegar, and sugar together in a medium bowl. Trim the scallions and slice them thin, keeping the green and white parts separate. Add the scallion greens to the bowl.

2 Heat the vegetable oil in a large skillet over medium heat until rippling. Add the scallion whites, ginger, and garlic. Stir just until you can smell the garlic, about 30 seconds. Add the broccoli slaw mix and toss until the broccoli turns bright green. Season with salt and transfer into the bowl of dressing. Toss well to mix, season with salt, and toss again. Keep at room temperature, tossing occasionally, for up to 4 hours. Leftovers may be refrigerated, but bring them to room temperature before serving.

Orange-Honey-Glazed Roasted Brussels Sprouts

Orange juice gets a sweetness boost from honey and an attitude adjustment from soy sauce. The result is a bright, savory brussels sprouts dish.

MAKES: ABOUT 3 CUPS, OR 4 SERVINGS • PREP TIME: 15 MINUTES • COOK TIME: 40 MINUTES

1 pound large brussels sprouts

2 tablespoons vegetable oil

Salt and several grinds of black pepper

⅓ cup bottled not-from-concentrate orange juice

1½ tablespoons honey of your choice

1½ teaspoons soy sauce

1 Preheat the oven to 400°F with a rack in the center position.

2 Trim the root ends from the sprouts, then cut the sprouts in quarters (halves if smaller). Toss them onto a half sheet pan (13 x 18-inch or similar size) as you go. When all the sprouts are trimmed, drizzle them with the oil and sprinkle them with salt and pepper. Toss them well with your hands to coat with oil and seasoning. Roast until tender and well browned, stirring around a few times, about 30 minutes.

3 Meanwhile, whisk the orange juice, honey, and soy sauce together in a small saucepan. Bring to a boil and continue to boil until reduced to about 3 tablespoons and syrupy. Set aside.

4 Pour the orange-honey glaze over the hot, tender sprouts, toss well to coat, and return to the oven for 3 to 4 minutes to heat the glaze. Spoon into a serving dish and serve hot or at room temperature.

Lemon-Basil Cooler (With or Without Booze)

Perfect for out on the lanai, whether grilling, looking for UFOs, or just hanging out.

MAKES: 2 CUPS SYRUP, ENOUGH FOR 8 COOLERS • PREP TIME: 15 MINUTES (PLUS COOLING TIME)

1½ cups cold water

⅓ cup sugar

1½ packed cups basil leaves and stems

½ cup freshly squeezed lemon juice

Club soda, seltzer, or sparkling water

Vodka or clear rum (optional)

1 Heat the cold water and sugar to a boil in a small saucepan over low heat, stirring to dissolve the sugar. Drop in the basil, remove the pan from the heat, and cool/steep for about 1 hour.

2 Stir in the lemon juice and strain the syrup. Refrigerate until chilled. The syrup can be stored, tightly covered, in the refrigerator for a week or two.

3 To make a cooler: Fill a tall glass with ice. Pour in about ¼ cup of the lemon-basil syrup. Fill with sparkling water, club soda, or seltzer. Garnish with a sprig of basil and a lemon slice if you like. To make a spiked cooler, add vodka or rum along with the syrup.

Whole-Wheat Oatmeal Raisin Cookies

These oat-y, buttery treats are, like most homemade cookies, best eaten warm. Rose loves them with a cold glass of milk; Dorothy has them with a cup of coffee or strong Earl Grey tea.

MAKES: ABOUT 20 COOKIES • PREP TIME: 10 MINUTES • BAKE TIME: 12 TO 14 MINUTES ─────

1½ cups old-fashioned (not instant) oats

¾ cup white whole-wheat flour or ¼ cup all-purpose flour plus ½ cup whole-wheat flour

¾ cup raisins

¾ teaspoon baking powder

¼ teaspoon salt

1 stick unsalted butter, at room temperature

¾ cup light brown sugar

1 egg

1 teaspoon vanilla extract

1 Preheat the oven to 350°F. Line one (or two if you have them) baking sheets with parchment paper or spray them with nonstick cooking spray.

2 Stir the oats, flour, raisins, baking powder, and salt together in a medium bowl.

3 Using a handheld electric mixer, beat the butter and sugar together in a medium bowl until fluffy—the butter will take on a lighter color. Beat in the egg together with the vanilla. Stir the oat mixture into the butter mixture by hand.

4 Use a tablespoon to scoop and drop the batter by slightly mounded spoonfuls onto the prepared baking sheets. Bake until lightly browned on the bottom, 12 to 14 minutes.

Berry-Almond Shortcake

Here's an example where leaving things a little rough leads to a very elegant dessert. Craggy, barely sweet shortcakes filled with juicy berries and topped with whipped cream are the height of elegance, like one of Dorothy's no-holds-barred date-night outfits.

MAKES: 4 SERVINGS • PREP TIME: 20 MINUTES • BAKE TIME: 20 MINUTES

FOR THE SHORTCAKE:

1½ cups unbleached all-purpose flour, plus a little more for the finished dough

½ cup toasted slivered almonds

1½ tablespoons sugar

1 teaspoon baking powder

½ teaspoon baking soda

¼ teaspoon salt

4 tablespoons unsalted butter, cut into 4 pieces and well chilled

⅔ cup chilled buttermilk

BAKE THE SHORTCAKES:

1 Preheat the oven to 450°F. Line a baking sheet with parchment paper or a silicone mat, or spray the sheet with nonstick cooking spray.

2 Buzz the flour and 6 tablespoons of the almonds in a food processor just until the almonds are very finely chopped. Don't overdo it; you should still feel finely ground almonds when you rub the flour between your fingertips.

3 Scrape the flour-almond mixture into a medium bowl and stir in the sugar, baking powder, baking soda, and salt. Work the butter into the flour mixture with your fingertips or a pastry blender until the butter is the size of tiny peas. Drizzle the buttermilk into the flour mixture, tossing gently with a fork. The dough should barely hold together. Turn the dough out onto a clean and lightly floured countertop. Knead the dough gently and just a few times—and when Dorothy says "gently and just a few times," she means it!—until any loose bits of flour are incorporated into the dough.

4 Divide the dough into 4 equal pieces. Without shaping them or working the dough too much, get the dough pieces onto the prepared baking sheet. Pat them very gently into irregular circles about 1½ inches high. They should look rough around the edges (and tops!). Their individuality is what makes them special—these are shortcakes, not Rockettes.

5 Scatter the remaining 2 tablespoons of almonds over the tops. Bake until risen and golden brown, about 20 minutes. Cool on a wire rack.

FOR THE BERRIES:

4 to 5 cups berries: raspberries, blackberries, cut-up strawberries, or a mix of the three

1½ tablespoons sugar

A few drops lemon juice

Whipped cream, sweetened or unsweetened, if you like

PREP THE BERRIES:

6 While the shortcakes are baking and cooling, toss the berries, sugar, and lemon juice together in a medium bowl. Let stand, tossing once in a while, until the shortcakes are cool. Nice, ripe berries will give off juices that will soak into the shortcake.

7 When the shortcakes are cool, split them in half using a fork (like an English muffin)—carefully, they're crumbly—and transfer to plates. Lift the tops, spoon some of the berries and juice over the bottoms, and replace the tops. Serve right away, with whipped cream if you like. If serving with whipped cream, save a little of the berry juices and drizzle those over the whipped cream.

—————— GOLDEN WISDOM ——————

Let the shortcakes cool before splitting and filling them, but don't wait until they're cold. They will dry out and lose their fabulous crust quickly.

Dorothy's Chocolate or Vanilla Malts

As Dorothy can tell you, nothing beats sipping the last of a malted milkshake out of the blender—or, like when Dorothy was in the malted milk trade, the bottom of the mixer cup. Well, maybe there is one thing—drinking the rest of the malt out of a tall, frosty glass.

MAKES: 1 MALT • PREP TIME: 5 MINUTES

2 scoops (1 cup) vanilla or chocolate ice cream

¾ cup whole milk

2 tablespoons malted milk powder (see notes)

½ teaspoon vanilla extract

Pinch salt

Combine all ingredients in a blender jar or the cup of a malted milk mixer. Start on low speed and blend until the ice cream is mostly melted. Increase the speed and mix until the malt is smooth and frosty. Pour into a tall chilled glass and enjoy!

Notes: This recipe can be easily doubled if the blender is large enough.

If you're really into malted milk, take a little time to search out malted milk powder that lists barley malt or malted barley as the first ingredient. It's easy to find online or in baking supply stores.

Crazy Coconut-Chocolate Clusters

These started out as macaroons, but Dorothy, as thrifty as she is practical, found a few mini chocolate chips in the cupboard and decided "What the heck!" These will last for days, if you keep them hidden. Try popping one in the freezer for five minutes before savoring it—a real treat!

MAKES: ABOUT 18 2-INCH CLUSTERS • PREP TIME: 15 MINUTES • COOK TIME: 35 MINUTES

2½ cups unsweetened coconut flakes

⅓ cup mini chocolate chips

2 egg whites

Large pinch salt

3 tablespoons sugar

3 tablespoons sweetened condensed milk

½ teaspoon vanilla extract

1 Heat the oven to 350°F.

2 Spread half (1¼ cups) of the coconut on a baking sheet and bake until the coconut is evenly and lightly browned, about 5 minutes. Stir the coconut once about halfway through to make sure it browns evenly. Turn the oven temperature down to 300°F. Cool the coconut and baking sheet completely.

3 Stir the toasted and untoasted coconut and the chocolate chips together in a medium bowl. Beat the whites and salt together in a small bowl. When the whites are foamy, start adding the sugar gradually. Beat until the meringue holds soft peaks. Stir in the condensed milk and vanilla and then stir the meringue mixture into the coconut mixture.

4 Line the cooled baking sheet with a silicone baking mat or parchment sheet. Drop the batter by mounded teaspoons, making irregular-looking mounds (better tall than flat). Bake until the meringue is browned and a cluster feels light when you pick it up, about 35 minutes. Cool 5 minutes, then transfer the clusters to a cooling rack and cool completely. Now there is a serious choice to be made: leave the clusters out, uncovered, for a chewy texture, or store them in a covered container for a more crumbly texture. Either way, they won't last long.

Mr. Ha Ha's New York–Style Birthday Mini-Cheesecake Cupcakes

If Dorothy had known these were on the menu at Mr. Ha Ha's Hacienda Hut, she might have been able to weather her birthday luncheon with Rose and Blanche a little better.

MAKES: ABOUT 24 SMALL (2-INCH) CUPCAKES • PREP TIME: 40 MINUTES • COOK TIME: 40 MINUTES (PLUS CHILL TIME)

FOR THE CRUST:

9 ounces graham crackers (about 16 whole crackers)

½ cup sugar

½ teaspoon salt

9 tablespoons unsalted butter, melted and cooled

MAKE AND FORM THE CRUST:

1 Crumble the graham crackers into the food processor. Pulse until coarsely chopped. (Work with half the graham crackers at a time if your processor isn't large enough to hold them in one batch.) Add the sugar and salt and process until the crackers are finely ground. Pour in the melted butter and process, scraping down the sides of the processor a few times, until the butter is completely mixed in and the crumb mixture looks like very wet, fine sand. Scrape the crumb mix into a bowl and, if necessary, cool to room temperature.

2 Press 2 tablespoons of the crumb mixture into each of the 24 small silicone baking cups (see notes), pressing it firmly against the bottom and sides. Don't worry if the sides aren't perfectly even. Set the filled cups on a baking sheet as you work. If you don't have enough cups to use up all the crust mix, bake the cupcakes in two batches. Chill the lined cups until needed.

Notes: Silicone baking cups come in different sizes. For a yield of 24 two-to-three bite cupcakes (as here), use cups that are about 2½ inches across the top and 1¼ inches high. Larger cups will, of course, make bigger but fewer cupcakes.

The crust mix and the filling mix each make about 3 cups. Depending on the size and shape of your baking cups, you may have a little of one or the other left over. Leftover crumbs make a good ice-cream topping. Bake leftover filling in the same cups without crusts.

FOR THE FILLING:

1 pound cream cheese, at room temperature and soft

½ cup sugar

1½ teaspoons cornstarch

1 egg + 1 yolk

½ teaspoon vanilla extract

¼ cup full-fat or reduced-fat sour cream

¾ teaspoon finely grated orange zest

¾ teaspoon finely grated lemon zest

MAKE THE FILLING:

3 Heat the oven to 350°F.

4 Using a handheld or stand mixer, beat the cream cheese, sugar, and cornstarch together until creamy, stopping to scrape down the sides of the bowl a few times. Beat in the egg and yolk, stopping once to scrape the sides and bottom of the bowl. Beat in the vanilla. Switch to the spatula and stir in the sour cream and both zests.

5 Divide the filling evenly among the cups on the baking sheet. (The filling shouldn't come above the edge of the crust.) Put the pan in the oven. Immediately turn down the heat to 300°F. Bake until the centers are firm, about 35 minutes. Remove and cool to room temperature. With your fingertip, gently brush any crust that extends over the cheesecake filling onto the baking sheet. Gather up the crumbs and sprinkle them over the tops of the cupcakes. Refrigerate the cupcakes, right on the baking sheet, until firm to the touch, about an hour.

6 Peel back the cups from the cupcakes and line them up on a clean baking sheet. Repeat with the remaining crust mix and filling if necessary. Serve chilled or remove to room temperature for 30 minutes before serving. Serve the cupcakes on a platter, cake stands, or a number of small plates. Any extra cheesecake cupcakes can be packed in an airtight container and refrigerated for up to 3 days or frozen for up to 1 month.

— GOLDEN WISDOM —

Avoid adding the zests to the batter while using the mixer; most of zest will end up stuck to the beaters or clumped together in the bowl.

And now it's time for the Mr. Ha Ha Birthday Roundup! When I call your name, please come up onstage!

Mr. Ha Ha

Patty Spina!

Please say you didn't do this!

(to Rose)

Jeannie Taylor!

Please tell me you didn't do this!

(to Rose)

Dorothy Zbornak!

Dorothy, you're making a fool of yourself! Mr. Ha Ha's looking at you!

(to Dorothy as she's throttling Rose)

Are you Dorothy Zbornak?

That's right.

Get up onstage, Dorothy!

Get bent, Ha Ha!

Rose

> It's like we say in St. Olaf: Christmas without fruitcake is like St. Sigmund's Day without the headless boy.

Like everything else in her life, Rose's choices in the kitchen are a mix of the truly absurd and the downright practical. Recipes that harken back to life in St. Olaf are a big part of Rose's repertoire.

And while it's true you might not have a craving for Candied Herring or a Maple Syrup-Honey-Brown Sugar-Molasses-Rice Krispies Log, you may find some of Rose's less offbeat dishes, like Lindstrom Surprise or Sperhüven Krispies, exciting—especially since they've been tweaked a bit for more refined palates.

Rose's cooking is perfect for hearty appetites. One example is her farm-style breakfast: golden, tender omelets, crispy home fries, and multigrain pancakes. Individual Quick-Fix Chicken Pot Pies can be made for a weeknight dinner, and still give you time to change out of your work clothes and into your duck sweater. Sour-Creamed Spinach and Dilled New Potatoes would balance out (and taste great) next to Swedish Meatballs or a simple steak grilled out on the lanai.

Entertaining? Staging a fake wake for an elderly friend? Rose has the answer: Arrange platters of gorgeous two-bite-size open sandwiches with flavors that pull from Rose's Scandinavian heritage, including dill, sour cream, salmon, herring, ham, and dense, boldly flavored bread. Top it all off with a Lingonberry Trifle and everybody goes home happy. Make the Cheese Puffs and Minnesota Antifreeze for the triplets from St. Olaf.

Rose's most beloved recipe is her Vänskapskaka . . . also known as St. Olaf Friendship Cake. Surely, there's no one in your life who wouldn't appreciate a Vänskapskaka —except, possibly, the one guy in the office who truly can't stand you. Give it to someone else.

Multigrain Pancake Mix

Part of a big farm-style breakfast, like the one Rose made for Dorothy's friend Jean when she came to visit. Rose still has her grandmother's heavy cast-iron griddle, which she heats up on the stovetop for these pancakes. She believes it is the best way to make pancakes. She's right.

MAKES: 6 CUPS BATTER, 12 6-INCH PANCAKES • PREP TIME: 5 MINUTES FOR MIX • COOK TIME: 10 MINUTES

FOR THE MIX:
2 cups old-fashioned oats

⅓ cup light or dark brown sugar

2 cups all-purpose flour

¾ cup buckwheat flour

¾ cup fine cornmeal

1 cup white whole-wheat flour

1 tablespoon baking powder

1 teaspoon baking soda

FOR EACH BATCH:
1½ cups buttermilk*

1 egg

1 tablespoon vegetable oil

Rose strongly suggests the grated zest of half an orange (and who are we to argue with Rose?)

Big pinch salt

1¾ cups pancake mix

Unsalted butter or nonstick cooking spray

TO SERVE:
Maple syrup, lingonberry preserves, or the jam or jelly of your choice

Confectioners' sugar (optional)

FOR THE MIX:

1 Whir the oats and brown sugar in a food processor until the oats are finely chopped. (Don't overprocess to a powder.) Transfer the oat mixture into a large bowl and add the all-purpose flour, buckwheat flour, cornmeal, white whole-wheat flour, baking powder, and baking soda. Whisk until evenly blended. Store the mix in a tightly sealed container for up to two months, or three in the fridge.

FOR EACH BATCH:

2 Beat the buttermilk, egg, vegetable oil, and salt together until the yolk is completely blended into the milk. Add the orange zest and dry mix and stir just until the ingredients are blended. Let stand for 15 to 30 minutes at room temperature.

3 Heat a heavy griddle, cast-iron skillet, or nonstick pan over medium-high heat until a few drops of water flicked from your fingers dance for a second and evaporate almost immediately. Add the butter to the pan or spray with the cooking spray. Ladle ½ cup of the batter onto the griddle for each pancake. Make only as many pancakes as will fit on the griddle comfortably without touching. Cook until the bottoms are a deep, lacy golden brown, about 3 minutes (lift an edge of one or two of the pancakes to peek). Flip the pancakes and cook until the second side is light golden brown (they won't be lacy like the first side) and feels springy to the touch, about 3 minutes. Serve hot and then make the next batch. The pancake maker eats last, proving that all good things come to those who wait.

*If you do not have buttermilk
on hand, mix 1 cup 2% milk and
½ cup plain yogurt until blended.

Farmstead Omelet

Growing up on a farm meant hearty breakfasts for Rose and her family: usually pancakes (page 56), bacon, and golden omelets with eggs gathered fresh from the henhouse. Count Bessie, being a showbiz chicken, was exempt from laying. She needed her rest and plenty of time for rehearsals. "Old MacDonald" is one of the most demanding tunes for an aspiring chicken star.

MAKES: 1 OMELET • PREP TIME: 5 MINUTES • COOK TIME: 5 MINUTES

3 eggs

½ teaspoon salt

2 teaspoons butter

Filling of your choice (see below for some ideas)

FILLINGS (Use any one or a mix of two or more; If mixing, use about 1/3 cup filling per omelet):

¼ cup cooked and crumbled bacon

½ cup sautéed mushrooms

¼ cup baby peas

½ cup diced ham and sautéed bell pepper

⅓ cup shredded cheese, such as Swiss, cheddar, Monterey Jack, or crumbled feta

Beat the eggs, 2 teaspoons water, and the salt together in a bowl until very well blended. Melt the butter in a nonstick omelet pan, preferably 6 inches across the bottom, over medium-low heat. When it is foaming—don't let the butter brown—pour in the egg mixture. Let the eggs sit until they are cooked around the top edges, about 30 seconds or so. With a heatproof rubber spatula, push the cooked edges gently down the sides of the pan, allowing the runny egg to fill in the space around the edges. Repeat every time the edges are cooked around the edges, tilting the pan as necessary to get all of the runny egg down to the hot pan. When no more runny egg moves off the top and into the pan, the top will still be runny. If this is how you like your eggs, simply top one half of the omelet with the filling, fold the other half over the filling, and slide onto a plate. For a medium-cooked omelet with less runny filling, add the filling and fold to close, then keep the omelet in the pan for 1 minute, flipping once. For a well-done omelet with no runny center, keep the omelet in the pan for 2 minutes, flipping once.

GOLDEN WISDOM

Have fun with fillings and use leftovers and odds and ends instead of more traditional options (be sure to warm them first). Try a half cup of leftover turkey stuffing (don't knock it till you've tried it!), macaroni and cheese, or Chinese takeout chicken with broccoli.

Classic Home Fries

Not just for breakfast! Serve them with roast chicken, meat loaf, or a burger. These were definitely on Rose's breakfast menu when Dorothy's friend Jean came to visit the girls and fell hard for Rose, much to Blanche's surprise.

MAKES: 2 SERVINGS • PREP TIME: 10 MINUTES • COOK TIME: 15 MINUTES

1 tablespoon vegetable oil

1 medium yellow onion, diced into ½-inch pieces

1 tablespoon butter

1 large baked Russet potato, cut into ¾-inch chunks

Fine sea or kosher salt and freshly ground black pepper

1 Heat the vegetable oil in a large skillet over medium-low heat. Add the onion and cook, stirring occasionally, until light golden brown, about 6 minutes. Add the butter and, when it has melted, the potatoes. Season lightly with salt and pepper and gently stir, occasionally, until the potatoes are browned and crisp on the outside and fluffy on the inside, about 15 minutes. Adjust the heat as you cook so the bits of onion don't burn. Go by the sound; you should hear a mild protest coming from the potatoes, not an all-out frenzy.

2 If serving right away, dish out the home fries right from the skillet. If serving later, spread the home fries out on a baking sheet and rewarm them in a 450°F oven, turning once, until heated through and re-crisped, about 5 minutes.

GOLDEN WISDOM

To double the yield, simply make two batches, one after the other. Keep the first batch warm in a 200°F oven while the second batch cooks. Or, if you have two large skillets, fry both batches at the same time.

Bacon-Lettuce-Potato Sandwiches

It may sound like one of Rose's crazy St. Olaf dishes, but these are actually quite good. These sandwiches helped Sophia and Rose hold their own against their fiercest lunch wagon competition: Johnny No-Thumbs.

MAKES: 2 SANDWICHES • PREP TIME: 15 MINUTES • COOK AND REST TIME: 55 MINUTES (UNSUPERVISED)

1 large (8-ounce) red or Yukon Gold potato

1 tablespoon olive oil

1 teaspoon fresh thyme leaves or ½ teaspoon dried thyme

Coarse sea or kosher salt and freshly ground black pepper

6 thick slices bacon

4 slices of dense grain bread, or rolls, lengths of baguette, or whatever you like to build a sandwich on

Mayonnaise or mustard, or both

3 to 4 large leaves of romaine, thicker center stems removed and cut into sandwich-size lengths

1 Heat the oven to 400°F with a rack in the center position.

2 Scrub the potato but leave the skin on. Cut the potato into ½-inch slices. Toss the slices, olive oil, and thyme together in a small bowl. Lay out the potato slices on one end of a nonstick or parchment paper-lined baking sheet and sprinkle them with salt and pepper.

3 Lay out the bacon slices, barely touching, on the other end of the baking sheet. Bake until the bacon is browned but not overly crisp, about 14 minutes. Remove the bacon and drain on paper towels. Continue cooking the potatoes until they are very tender and golden brown around the edges, another 5 to 10 minutes. If you see the bacon and potatoes are cooking unevenly, rotate the pan halfway through the cooking. Cool the potatoes to room temperature.

4 Make the sandwiches: Toast the bread slices (or other bread) and generously spread all slices with mayonnaise and/or mustard. Stack the potatoes, bacon slices, and lettuce leaves over two of the bread slices and cap with the other slices. Cut in half—triangles or rectangles, it's your call—and enjoy!

Note: You may cook the bacon and potatoes hours ahead and keep at room temperature, but do not refrigerate them.

Scandinavian Style Open-Face Sandwiches

The Danes rule the roost when it comes to smørrebørd—open-face, beautifully constructed sandwiches. The Danes also have a lot of dos and don'ts regarding smørrebørd, but Rose, being from Minnesota, does not. Rose sticks to traditional ingredients like ham, herring, dill butter, and vegetable garnishes, but mixes and matches them in ways that seem right (and fun) to her. Please do the same.

The amounts given below for spreads and toppings will easily butter and top 40 to 50 mini sandwiches or 6 to 8 large sandwiches.

A FEW OPEN-FACE SANDWICH POINTERS

Traditionally, smørrebørd are large and made on whole slices of bread for a knife-and-fork meal. They are works of art and, when the Danes get involved, they can be works of art with some pretty strict rules. Rose loves to make small hors d'oeuvre–size sandwiches instead of the larger version and to thumb her nose—politely—at the rules. These instructions are for making small cocktail sandwiches, but you can certainly use the breads, spreads, sauces, toppings, and garnishes listed below to make full-meal sandwiches if you like.

The spreads, toppings, and garnishes can be made from hours to a day in advance. However, assembling the sandwiches should be done no more than an hour before serving.

Whether making a few large sandwiches or dozens of minis, first spread all the bread (except if making herring sandwiches) with dill butter. Next add the toppings of your choice. If you're using more than one type of bread, make sure to mix and match breads and toppings. Finish off the sandwiches with the garnishes, keeping in mind which go well with each topping and also what looks pretty.

BREADS

Thin slices of dense grain, rye, or pumpernickel bread

Whole slices of cocktail party rye or pumpernickel bread

Whole-grain bread, lightly toasted and cut into squares or triangles

BREAD SPREADS

The classic spread is dill butter, but store-bought fig spread is another great choice. (This is scrumptious with the blue cheese/apple/bacon combo and ham and Havarti number. No, it's not at all Scandinavian, but back in St. Olaf, Helga Flugentreble had a fig tree. . . .)

DILL BUTTER   Makes a generous ½ cup

Spread dill butter on bread for all these sandwiches except the creamed herring—the cream adds enough moistness and flavor of its own. Leftover dill butter is fantastic on baked or mashed potatoes, to butter the pan for scrambled eggs, or to stir into soups.

1 stick (4 ounces) unsalted butter, at room temperature and very soft

3 lightly packed tablespoons chopped fresh dill

1 teaspoon freshly squeezed lemon juice

¼ teaspoon fine sea salt

Few grinds black pepper

Whisk all ingredients together in a small bowl until the dill is mixed in evenly and the lemon juice is absorbed by the butter. Cover the bowl and keep at room temperature for up to 4 hours or refrigerate for several days. Soften the butter thoroughly at room temperature before using.

TOPPINGS

Sliced creamed herring
Thinly sliced rare roast beef
Tiny shrimp, tossed with a small dab of mayo, and seasoned with salt and pepper
Thinly sliced gravlax or smoked salmon
Danish blue cheese
Havarti cheese, plain or seasoned with caraway seeds

RÉMOULADE SAUCE   Makes about ⅔ cup

Leftover rémoulade makes a good all-purpose sandwich or hamburger topper.

½ cup homemade or good-quality store-bought mayonnaise, such as Sir Kensington's mayonnaise

1 heaping tablespoon drained capers, finely chopped

1 tablespoon minced cornichons or dill pickle

2 tablespoons minced shallot or red onion

1 tablespoon chopped fresh parsley (optional)

Freshly squeezed lemon juice, if needed

Stir all ingredients except the lemon juice together in a small bowl. Taste and add as much lemon juice as you like, or none. Cover and refrigerate until needed.

HORSERADISH CREAM SAUCE   Makes ½ cup

If possible, go for the red horseradish (colored with beets). The shocking pink color of the finished cream makes for a very pretty sandwich.

½ cup (4 ounces) full-fat sour cream

2 tablespoons red or white horseradish, with liquid

Fine sea salt and a few grinds black pepper to taste

Stir all ingredients together in a small bowl. Cover and refrigerate until needed and up to 3 days. Bring to room temperature and stir before using.

GARNISHES
(Have at least 6 to 8 of the following on hand—the more the merrier!)

Prepare up to one day before; lay out on a paper towel–lined baking sheet, cover with damp paper towels, and refrigerate:

Very thinly sliced red onion

Thinly sliced scallion

Dill sprigs

Cornichon fans (see photo)

Microgreens (best approach: pick through a small pack of spring mix to find an assortment of tiny leaves of different colors, shapes, and textures)

Cucumber ribbons (thin, long slices of cucumber, made with a vegetable peeler; cut to size according to sandwich)

Prepare several hours in advance and keep at room temperature:
Bacon, cooked crisp and crumbled or cut into 1-inch lengths before cooking

Walnut pieces, toasted and finely chopped

Halved cherry tomatoes

Green apple, very thinly sliced or finely diced, rubbed/tossed with lemon juice to prevent browning

SOME PARTICULARLY GOOD COMBOS (ALL ON DILL-BUTTERED BREAD):
Dark Swedish-style pumpernickel bread, roast beef, cornichon fans, and a dab of horseradish cream

Light Swedish-style rye, gravlax, cucumber ribbons, dill sprigs, and thinly sliced red onions

Party pumpernickel, fig spread, Danish blue cheese, apple, toasted walnut, and bacon

Tiny shrimp salad, halved cherry tomatoes, sliced scallion, and a dab of horseradish cream

Ham, cornichon fans, radicchio, and green apple

In addition to these suggested combinations, let your own taste be your guide and pair spreads, toppings, and garnishes according to what seems good to you!

Cheese Puffs

After a failed attempt to make lutefisk puffs a mainstay at get-togethers, Rose decided on these cheese puffs instead. This recipe makes enough to serve 8 to 10 large puffs warm from the oven, plus another 8 or so to freeze for on-the-spot hospitality—after all, neither Rose nor any of the girls knows when someone might stop by. And that someone could be an attorney delivering a pig, cousin Sven, or even an old boyfriend from St. Olaf who doesn't know how to kiss.

MAKES: ABOUT 20 LARGE PUFFS • PREP TIME: 25 MINUTES • BAKE TIME: 25 TO 30 MINUTES

½ cup water

½ cup whole milk

6 tablespoons unsalted butter

1 teaspoon kosher salt

1 cup all-purpose flour

4 large eggs

¾ cup shredded gruyere, plus a little more for tops of the puffs

1 Heat the oven to 425°F with a rack in the center position. Line 2 large baking sheets with parchment paper or silicone baking mats. If you plan to freeze half the batch (see notes), make sure at least one of the baking sheets fits in your freezer.

2 Heat the water, milk, butter, and salt in a medium-sized, heavy saucepan until the butter is melted and the water just comes to a boil. Turn the heat to medium-low, add the flour all at once, and beat until the dough is very thick and pulls away from the sides of the pan, about 2 minutes. Continue to beat until the dough stays in the center of the pan and starts to gather around the spoon.

3 Add the eggs to the pan, one at a time, beating very well after each. At first, it will seem as though the eggs won't mix with the batter. But continue beating, paying attention to the sides of the pan, until the batter is smooth after each egg is added. If you are ever in doubt, beat for a minute or two more.

4 Beat in ¾ cup gruyere. Drop the batter onto the prepared baking sheets by mounded tablespoons to form 1½- to 2-inch puffs. Top the puffs with the remaining cheese. Bake one or both trays for 5 minutes, reduce temp to 375°F, and continue baking until deep golden brown and the puffs feel very light when picked up from the sheet, 20 to 25 minutes longer. Rotate the sheets front to back and top to bottom on the oven racks halfway through cooking.

5 Poke the top of each puff with the tip of a paring knife to make a very small vent. Turn off the oven, close the door, and let the puffs sit 5 minutes. Serve right away or keep at room temperature to reheat later (see notes).

Notes:

Make the dough ahead: The dough can be prepared completely and stored in the refrigerator for up to 1 day. Form the puffs, top with cheese, and bake as above.

Freeze the puffs and bake later: Prepare the dough and form the puffs as above. Freeze all or part of a batch right on the baking sheets. When fully frozen, transfer the puffs to a resealable plastic bag. Bake right out of the freezer for a minute or two longer than puffs that haven't been frozen.

Reheat baked puffs: Baked puffs may be stored at room temperature for up to a few hours. About 15 minutes before serving, heat the oven to 350°F. Rewarm the puffs about 5 minutes or until heated through and firm on the outside.

Excuse me, I couldn't help but notice you took several of my tasty, delicious lutefisk puffs and you've hardly touched them.

Uh, I just don't care for them.

Eva

Yeah, well, that's an ugly hat!

Alma's Yellow Split Pea Soup

Rose's mom, Alma, learned a lot more on the farm than how to play poker and carve a gun out of soap. She also learned how to make hearty soups in big enough quantities to freeze some for another meal. When "winter" comes to Florida, Rose digs out this recipe and brings a little bit of Minnesota dairy-farm life to the girls' Miami kitchen. The lemon wedges were Blanche's idea.

MAKES: ABOUT 10 CUPS • PREP TIME: 15 MINUTES • COOK TIME: 1 HOUR 15 MINUTES

2 tablespoons unsalted butter, plus more for the soup, if you like

Bone from one semi-boneless smoked ham (such as a spiral-cut ham), with meat attached, or 3 large ham hocks

2 ribs celery, trimmed and diced

1 medium onion, peeled and diced

1 medium carrot, peeled and diced into ¼ inch pieces

1 pound split yellow peas

6 cups Rotisserie Chicken Broth (page 71) or store-bought reduced sodium chicken broth

Freshly ground black pepper and salt, if necessary, to taste

Lemon wedges

Note: If you have any leftover ham, cut it into cubes and add along with the meat from the bone in step 6.

1 Heat the butter in a 5-quart pot over low heat until melted. Add the bone or ham hocks and cook, turning frequently, until lightly browned on all sides, about 10 minutes.

2 Add the celery, onion, and carrot to the pot. Cook, stirring occasionally, until softened, about 10 minutes.

3 Meanwhile, rinse the peas in a sieve under cold running water, picking through them to remove any off-color or shriveled peas. Drain the peas.

4 Add the peas and broth to the pot, increase the heat to medium, and heat to boiling. Reduce the heat, cover the pot, and simmer, stirring occasionally, until the peas are tender, about 45 minutes. (There should always be enough liquid to cover the peas by about 1½ inches. If not, add broth or water as necessary.)

5 When the peas are tender, remove the bone or hocks to a plate. Customize the consistency of the soup by pureeing all or part of the soup in batches in a blender. (Pureeing all the soup will produce a very smooth soup, pureeing half the soup produces a slightly coarser soup, etc.) Return the soup to very low heat, thinning as necessary with additional broth or water.

6 Pick any ham from the bone or hocks and stir into the soup. Season the soup with freshly ground black pepper and salt to taste. Ladle into warmed bowls and garnish with a dab of butter if you like. Serve lemon wedges separately.

Rotisserie Chicken Broth

Making this broth—in about an hour—adds even more value to a store-bought rotisserie chicken. There will most likely be more broth than you need, yours to use in dishes like Baked Chickpea and Kale Casserole (page 36) or Swedish Meatballs (page 76).

MAKES: ABOUT 4 CUPS • PREP TIME: 10 MINUTES • COOK TIME: 1½ HOURS, UNATTENDED

1 store-bought rotisserie chicken

1 As you pick over the chicken for another recipe (such as Individual Quick-Fix Chicken Pot Pies, page 75), set aside all the bones and skin from the chicken. Get rid of any excess fat and, in short, anything that's not skin or bone. Put the picked-over goodness in a 3-quart pot and pour in enough cold water to cover. Bring to a boil over high heat, then adjust the heat so the broth is simmering. Cook for 1½ hours.

2 Let the broth cool a bit, then strain into a clean bowl. Cool before refrigerating. The broth will keep for up to 5 days in the refrigerator or up to a few months in the freezer. In either case, bring the broth to a boil before using.

I'm making Scandinavia's oldest and most traditional appetizer treat—cheese and crackers.

 Cheese and crackers, Rose? Not Eggs Gefluffen? Ham and Gunterhagens? Pigs in a Svengebluten?

No, but you sure know how to make a girl's mouth water.

Lindstrom Surprise

Another one of Rose's dishes that sounds wacky at first, but turns out to be rather delicious.

MAKES: 8 TO 12 SERVINGS • PREP TIME: 45 MINUTES, PLUS RESTING TIME • COOK TIME: 50 MINUTES

FOR THE PIE DOUGH:

3 cups all-purpose flour

½ teaspoon salt

8 tablespoons (1 stick) unsalted butter, cut into 8 pieces and chilled

4 tablespoons vegetable shortening, chilled

Large glass ice water (you'll need 7 to 8 tablespoons)

MAKE THE SAVORY PIE CRUST DOUGH:

1 Stir the flour and salt together in a large bowl. Add the butter and shortening and toss. Using a pastry blender or your fingertips, work the butter and shortening into the flour. With a pastry blender, repeatedly press down and occasionally scrape the sides of the bowl. With your fingertips, rub the pieces of butter and shortening together with the flour to break up the pieces. Either way, continue until the mix looks like very coarse cornmeal with an occasionally larger piece of fat. Refrigerate the mix for 15 minutes or so.

2 Sprinkle 6 tablespoons ice water over the flour mix, tossing with a fork at the same time, if you can manage it. If not, add/toss, add/toss, and so on. Toss until mixed well, then continue to add ice water, a little at a time, until the dough holds together when pressed with your fingertips. Add just enough water to hold the dough together without making it soggy. Turn the dough out onto the countertop and, working quickly, knead the dough very gently to incorporate any loose bits. Divide in half, wrap the halves in plastic wrap, and refrigerate for at least 30 minutes and up to 1 day.

I'm famous for my Lindstrom Surprise.

What in the world is that?

Herring pie. The surprise is you think it's pie, like apple, you know, but when you bite into it, it's herring!

Ha ha ha! What fun!

FOR THE FILLING:

2 tablespoons vegetable oil

2 medium red onions, cut into ¼-inch half-moon slices (about 4 loosely packed cups)

2 medium Yukon Gold potatoes (about 1 pound)

½ cup whole milk

½ cup full-fat sour cream

¼ pound marinated herring fillets (not herring in cream sauce), drained and cut into ½-inch pieces, about ⅓ cup

4 large scallions, trimmed and sliced thin (white and green parts)

¼ cup chopped parsley

¾ teaspoons fine sea or kosher salt, plus more for seasoning vegetables

Several grinds of black pepper

1 egg, beaten with a few drops of water

MAKE THE FILLING AND BAKE THE PIE:

3 Heat the oil over medium-low heat in a large, deep skillet with a lid. Stir in the onions, season lightly with salt, and cook, stirring, until softened, about 5 minutes.

4 Peel the potatoes. Cut them in half lengthwise and then into ¼-inch slices. Stir the potatoes into the skillet to separate the slices. Season again lightly with salt. Cover and cook, stirring occasionally, until the potatoes are half-tender. (You should be able to poke through the slices with some resistance.) Transfer the mixture to a bowl and cool to room temperature.

5 While the potato mixture is cooling, roll out one piece of the dough to a 12-inch circle on a lightly floured countertop. Fit into a 9-inch pie plate, pressing gently into the edges and making sure the overhang is even all the way around. Roll out the second half on the lightly floured countertop to an 11-inch circle and lay flat on a baking sheet. With the tip of a sharp knife or the narrow end of a plain ½-inch pastry tip, cut 5 to 6 small holes in the flat piece of dough. Chill both crusts for 30 minutes.

6 Stir the milk and sour cream into the onion-potato mixture to loosen it up. Stir in the herring, scallions, parsley, ½ teaspoon salt, and pepper. Mix gently but well. Taste and adjust the seasoning if needed.

7 Heat the oven to 375°F with a rack in the lower third position.

8 Spoon the filling into the pie pan and smooth into an even layer. Lay the top crust over the filling so the edges of the top and bottom crusts line up. Trim the crusts so they overhang the pie plate by ½ inch. Fold the edges of the top crust under the bottom crust to make a tight seal. Crimp the edges with the tines of a fork.

9 Brush the entire top of the pie lightly with the beaten egg. Bake 30 minutes. Rotate the pie front to back and continue baking until a little of the filling is bubbling up through the vents and the top is a rich golden brown, about 20 minutes longer. Cool at least 1 hour before serving. Serve warm or at room temperature. The pie may be refrigerated for up to 2 days. Warm in a 350°F oven for 15 minutes before serving.

Individual Quick-Fix Chicken Pot Pies

When the temperature dips below 70°F in Miami, Rose is ready with a cozy chicken pot pie that takes just minutes to get in the oven. With a prebaked crust of flaky puff pastry, the hot filling goes right from the pot to a serving bowl—no additional baking needed!

MAKES: 4 SERVINGS • PREP TIME: ABOUT 30 MINUTES • COOK TIME: 30 MINUTES

Half a 17½-ounce package puff pastry sheets, defrosted (see notes)

1 egg, well beaten with a few drops of water

3 cups Rotisserie Chicken Broth (page 71), or store-bought low-sodium broth

2 cups milk of your choice (whole, 2%, skim)

3 tablespoons unsalted butter

4 tablespoons all-purpose flour

2 teaspoons Worcestershire sauce

1½ teaspoons dried thyme

2 cups cubed cooked chicken, from a rotisserie chicken or other cooked chicken

3 cups cooked and diced or coarsely chopped vegetables (see notes)

Salt and freshly ground black pepper

1 Preheat the oven to 400°F.

2 Unfold the pastry onto a cutting board. Cut the pastry into 4 four-inch circles using biscuit cutters or a large glass. Poke each circle in several spots with a fork and place on a baking sheet. Brush the pastry circles generously with the beaten egg. Bake until puffed and deep golden brown, about 15 minutes.

3 Meanwhile, heat the broth and milk in a medium saucepan over low heat until steaming. In a separate large saucepan, melt the butter over medium heat. When foaming, add the flour and cook, stirring constantly, 4 minutes. Pour in 2 cups of the milk-broth mixture and bring to a boil, whisking constantly, paying attention to the bottom and sides of the pan. Slowly pour in the rest of the milk-broth mixture and heat to simmering. Whisk in the Worcestershire and thyme. Stir in the chicken and vegetables. Return to a simmer and season with salt and pepper.

4 Pour the chicken filling into 16-ounce crocks (large soufflé dishes work well). Top each crock with a circle of pastry and serve.

Notes: The most commonly sold puff pastry sheets, from Pepperidge Farm, come in a 17½-ounce package that contains two 9 x 9-inch pieces of dough. Use one for this recipe and save the other. Any other similar size piece of puff pastry will do.

Vary the vegetables according to your taste or what you have on hand. Add leftover baked potatoes, steamed broccoli, or string beans, or in a pinch, a bag of that old standby—peas and carrots—will do.

You can also make the pie in an 11 x 9-inch baking dish: Instead of cutting the pastry into circles, cut the sheet into 6 even rectangles. Poke, brush, and bake the pastry rectangles as described above. Pour filling into the baking dish. Overlap the baked pastry rectangles over the filling and serve a piece of pastry with each serving.

Swedish Meatballs

No, we're not talking about Rose and her St. Olaf neighbors, we're talking about the classic mix of pork-and-beef meatballs with a simple dill sauce. Roll them bigger for dinner and serve them with Dilled New Potatoes (page 83), or make them smaller to serve with drinks.

MAKES: 25 TO 50 MEATBALLS, DEPENDING ON SIZE • PREP TIME: 20 MINUTES • COOK TIME: 30 MINUTES ——————

FOR THE MEATBALLS:
1 tablespoon butter

1 cup finely chopped onion

¾ cup bread crumbs or panko

¼ cup milk (of any persuasion)

1 pound ground beef

1 pound ground pork

2 large eggs

1¼ teaspoons fine sea salt

½ teaspoon ground allspice or nutmeg

½ teaspoon ground black pepper

Vegetable oil, if browning on the stovetop

MAKE THE MEATBALLS:

1 Melt the butter in a medium sauté pan over low heat. Stir in the onion and cook, stirring occasionally, until the onion is softened but not browned, about 6 minutes. Meanwhile, pour the milk over the bread crumbs in a small bowl. Let stand, stirring once or twice, until you need them.

2 Crumble the ground beef and pork into a large bowl. Crack in the eggs and sprinkle the salt, allspice or nutmeg, and pepper over the meats. Add the softened onions and crumble the soaked crumbs into the bowl. Mix thoroughly with your hands until you can see the onions distributed throughout.

3 Form the meatballs into 1½-inch (¾-ounce) to 2-inch (1½-ounce) balls and line them up on a baking pan. To broil: Set a rack 4 to 5 inches from the broiler and preheat the broiler to high. Broil the meatballs, turning once, until well browned on both sides, about 8 minutes. To panfry: Pour about ¼ inch of vegetable oil into a large, heavy pan (cast-iron, anyone?). Heat over medium heat until the oil is shimmering. Add as many meatballs as will fit without crowding. Cook, turning occasionally, until well browned on all sides, about 10 minutes. Adjust the heat as you cook so the meatballs give off a lively sizzle but aren't splattering. Drain the browned meatballs on paper towels or a brown paper bag. Change the oil if you start to see burnt bits floating around in it. If you control the heat well, this shouldn't be an issue. Set them aside at room temperature while making the sauce.

FOR THE SAUCE:

2 tablespoons butter

2 tablespoons all-purpose flour

2 cups hot homemade chicken or beef broth, or store-bought reduced-sodium chicken or beef broth

Sea salt and freshly ground black pepper

¼ cup chopped fresh dill

2 tablespoons sour cream (optional)

MAKE THE SAUCE:

4   Melt the butter in a deep 9-inch sauté pan over medium-low heat. Stir in the flour. Cook, stirring, until the roux turns a very light brown. Pour a little of the hot broth into the pan and whisk until the sauce is smooth. Add the rest of the broth and whisk—paying attention to the corners—until smooth. Bring to a boil, adjust the heat to simmering, and cook 5 minutes, whisking several times. Add salt and pepper to taste.

5   Add the meatballs to the sauce and cover the sauté pan. Cook over low heat, shaking the pan occasionally, until the meatballs are heated through, about 5 minutes. Leave them this way if you're serving with rice, noodles, or mashed potatoes. If you'd like a thicker sauce that glazes the meatballs, turn the heat up a little and cook the sauce, rolling the meatballs around in it, about 10 minutes. In either case, remove the meatballs to a serving bowl and whisk the dill and sour cream, if using, into the sauce. Pour the sauce over the meatballs and serve.

"Le Trout"

Two 6- to 7-ounce trout fillets

Fine sea or kosher salt

¼ cup very fine yellow cornmeal

¼ cup all-purpose flour

2 tablespoons vegetable oil

2 tablespoons unsalted butter

¼ cup sliced almonds, preferably unpeeled

⅓ cup dry white wine

1 tablespoon lemon juice

2 tablespoons thinly sliced chives or chopped Italian parsley

1 Pat the trout fillets dry. Season both sides lightly with salt. Mix the cornmeal and flour on a baking sheet and dredge both sides of the fillets in the cornmeal mix. If you have the time, dry the trout fillets on a cooling rack for about 20 minutes. If not, they will still be delicious.

2 Heat the vegetable oil in a large skillet (the trout fillets should fit in easily with room to flip them over). When the oil is rippling, add the trout skin-side down and cook until well browned, 3 to 4 minutes. Adjust the heat so the trout is sizzling but not spattering. Carefully flip the trout and repeat. Remove the trout to baking sheet. (If you like, keep the trout warm in a 200°F oven.)

3 Pour off all but a very thin layer of oil from the pan and add 1 tablespoon of the butter, plus the almonds. Stir until the almonds are lightly browned. Pour in the wine. Bring to a boil, scraping the bottom of the pan. Boil until almost completely evaporated. Remove the pan from the heat and add the remaining 1 tablespoon butter, the lemon juice, and the chives or parsley. Swirl the pan until the sauce is well blended. If there is enough sauce to coat the fillets evenly, let it be. If you'd like a little more sauce, add about 1 tablespoon of water. Check the sauce for salt, pepper, and lemon, and add more of any you like.

4 Transfer the trout to 2 plates, then spoon the pan sauce over the fillets and around them. Serve right away.

How do you say "trout" in French?

Le trout.

Dr. Jonathan Newman

Sour-Creamed Spinach

No skimping on texture and flavor, this reduced-fat version of traditional creamed spinach is put together in minutes. Pairs very well with Swedish Meatballs (page 76) or Southern Not-Fried Chicken (page 116).

MAKES: 4 SERVINGS • PREP TIME: 10 MINUTES • COOK TIME: 20 MINUTES (UNATTENDED)

Two 10-ounce packages frozen chopped spinach, thawed

½ cup sour cream (full-fat or reduced-fat)

¼ cup milk

¾ teaspoon fine sea salt

½ teaspoon freshly ground black pepper

Pinch grated nutmeg

2 tablespoons grated Parmesan cheese

1 Heat the oven to 400°F with a rack in the top position.

2 Squeeze out the spinach with your hands to remove as much water as possible. Beat the sour cream, milk, salt, pepper, and nutmeg together in a medium bowl until blended. Add the spinach and stir until coated. Transfer the spinach to a small baking dish (about 8 x 5-inch) and coat the top with the Parmesan. Bake until the edges are bubbling and the cheese is browned, about 20 minutes. Let stand 5 minutes and serve hot.

GOLDEN WISDOM

The best way to defrost the spinach is to remove it from the freezer a day or two before using. Put the packages of spinach in a bowl in the refrigerator until thawed.

Dilled New Potatoes

So easy, Rose can make them in her sleep! The trick—as with anything this simple—is to make sure the ingredients are the best: potatoes that are as firm and "new" as possible, creamery butter, and bright fresh dill.

MAKES: 4 SERVINGS • PREP TIME: 5 MINUTES • COOK TIME: 20 MINUTES (MOSTLY UNATTENDED)

1 pound very small new potatoes—white, red, purple, or a mix of the three

1½ tablespoons unsalted butter

3 tablespoons (or more) chopped fresh dill

1 teaspoon lemon juice

Freshly ground black pepper

Coarse sea salt, such as Maldon

1 Scrub the potatoes and put them in a wide medium saucepan. It's helpful if the pan is the right size to hold the potatoes in one fairly tight layer. Pour in enough cold water to cover them by 1 inch. Bring to a boil over medium heat. Adjust the heat to a bare simmer and cook until the potatoes are just tender when poked with the tip of a knife—not long enough to split the skins or make them mushy. Timing will vary depending on the potatoes, from 12 minutes for tiny new potatoes to 20 minutes for larger spuds.

2 Drain the potatoes and return them to the pan. Let them stand uncovered for a couple of minutes. Their own heat and the heat from the pan will evaporate moisture and keep them from getting soggy. Add the butter, dill, lemon juice, and pepper. Roll them around to coat with the seasoned butter, then add enough coarse salt to season them.

Fluffy Tomato-Cuke Salad

Rose likes fluffy: fluffy sweaters, fluffy bunny slippers, cute fluffy animals. By adding some baby greens to a cucumber-tomato salad, she adds a little fluffiness here, too, not to mention flavor. It's a nice trick to know. Use it with regular green salads, too.

MAKES: 4 SERVINGS • PREP TIME: 15 MINUTES, PLUS 30 MINUTES UNATTENDED MARINATING TIME

1 cup cherry or grape tomatoes, the smaller the better, cut in half

2 mini (Persian or Kirby) cucumbers or half a large hothouse cucumber

½ teaspoon fine sea or kosher salt, plus more for seasoning

1 tablespoon olive oil

1 tablespoon mayonnaise

½ teaspoon Dijon mustard

2 cups baby arugula, baby kale, or other baby greens, washed and spun dry

1 Put the halved tomatoes in a medium bowl. Trim the ends off the cucumbers. Cut the cukes in quarters lengthwise, then crosswise into ½-inch pieces. Add them to the bowl with the tomatoes. Sprinkle ½ teaspoon salt over the vegetables and toss well. Let the vegetables stand, tossing once or twice, for 30 minutes.

2 Stir the olive oil, mayonnaise, and mustard into the cucumber and tomatoes, blending well. Add the greens, toss, and season with salt and pepper, if needed. Serve immediately.

Sperhüven Krispies

We couldn't get the secret recipe out of Rose, but here's our version of St. Olaf's legendary Sperhüven Krispies—a treat that tastes like "cheesecake, fresh strawberries, and chocolate ice cream," or close enough. And best of all, there's no baking . . . nor the horrible odor involved with the traditional version of Sperhüven Krispies.

MAKES: 24 SERVINGS • PREP TIME: 20 MINUTES, PLUS 20 MINUTES UNATTENDED COOLING TIME

FOR THE CHOCOLATY KRISPIES:
2 tablespoons unsalted butter

3 cups (half a 10-ounce bag) mini marshmallows

1 tablespoon unsweetened dark cocoa powder

3 cups Kellogg's Rice Krispies cereal

FOR THE CHEESECAKE ICING AND TOPPINGS:
¾ cup plain cream cheese, at room temperature

¼ cup confectioners' sugar

2 tablespoons full-fat or reduced-fat sour cream

½ teaspoon vanilla extract

Pinch of salt

About ⅓ cup mini chocolate chips

Strawberry jam or preserves

MAKE THE KRISPIES:

1 Melt the butter in a wide, heavy sauté pan over very low heat. Add the marshmallows, sprinkle the cocoa over them, and stir with a heatproof spatula until the marshmallows are completely melted. If the marshmallow/cocoa mixture begins to stick to the pan, use a metal spatula with a flat end to free it.

2 Stir the cereal into the marshmallow mix and stir gently, scraping the bottom of the pan until the cereal is coated with marshmallow cream, again using the flat metal spatula if needed. Scoop up a generous tablespoonful of the mix and set into a compartment of a mini muffin tin. Press the Krispie gently to flatten the top and fill the compartment evenly. Repeat with the remaining mix. Let set for 20 to 30 minutes.

MEANWHILE, MAKE THE ICING:

3 Beat the cream cheese, confectioners' sugar, sour cream, vanilla, and salt until very smooth. Set aside at room temperature.

FINISH UP THE KRISPIES:

4 When the Krispies are firm, loosen them from the muffin tin. Top each with just enough icing to cover the top. Line them up on a parchment- or waxed paper-lined tray as you go. Scatter enough chips over them to almost cover the tops. Using a ½-teaspoon measuring spoon, place a round dab of strawberry jam in the center of each Krispie. Chill for at least 1 hour and up to 8 hours before serving. If you like, gild the lily with a sprinkling of confectioners' sugar. Holding your nose is optional.

It's an ancient Scandinavian midnight snack.

Well, they smell god-awful.

Vänskapskaka . . . aka St. Olaf Friendship Cake

Oddly, for a dish with St. Olaf roots, this moist cake, baked with "milk, sugar, honey, a whole lot of love, and just a drop of sunshine," is a pretty straightforward recipe. Some of the honey settles to the bottom of the finished cake and creates a honey-infused layer of extra sweetness for your old or newfound friends to enjoy.

MAKES: ONE 9-INCH LOAF CAKE, OR 10 SERVINGS • PREP TIME: 20 MINUTES • BAKE TIME: 50 MINUTES

1¾ cups bleached all-purpose flour, plus more for the cake pan

1 teaspoon baking powder

½ teaspoon salt

½ cup sliced almonds

2 sticks plus 2 tablespoons unsalted butter, plus more for greasing the pan, at room temperature

¾ cup sugar

¼ cup honey

1 teaspoon almond extract

4 eggs

½ cup whole milk

Confectioners' sugar

1 Heat the oven to 325°F with a rack in the center position. Butter and flour a 9 x 5-inch loaf pan. Sift the flour, baking powder, and salt together onto a sheet of parchment paper or into a bowl. Set aside.

2 Toast the almonds on a baking sheet until very pale golden, about 8 minutes. Set aside.

3 Beat the butter until creamy. Add the sugar gradually, stopping occasionally to scrape the bottom and sides of the bowl. Add the honey and almond extract. Beat until well blended. Beat in the eggs one at a time, stopping twice to scrape down the sides and bottom of the bowl.

4 With the mixer on low speed, add half the dry ingredients to the bowl. When about half-blended, scrape the bottom and sides of the bowl and add the milk. When just a few streaks of flour remain, add the remaining dry ingredients. Scrape the bottom and sides of the bowl and mix just until no streaks of flour remain.

5 Scrape the batter into the prepared pan and smooth the top. Top evenly with the toasted almonds and bake until the top is golden brown and a wooden pick is withdrawn clean, about 50 minutes. Cool on a rack for 20 minutes. Turn the pan on its side and wiggle the cake out of the pan. Cool completely (overnight if possible). Sprinkle enough confectioners' sugar over the cake to almost completely cover the top and cut the cake into thick slices.

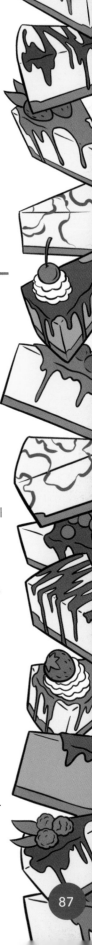

Lingonberry Trifle

Why do four Golden Girls need eight servings of trifle? Leftovers! If possible, make this a day in advance to give all the flavors and textures a chance to blend.

MAKES: 8 SERVINGS • PREP TIME: 20 MINUTES

Pastry Cream (page 90), chilled

One 14-ounce jar (scant 2 cups) lingonberry preserves or preserves of your choice

4 cups berries, e.g., whole raspberries or blackberries, or hulled and sliced strawberries

Lemon juice, if needed

Sugar, if needed

1 cup heavy cream, chilled

5 cups cubed (¾-inch) Friendship Cake (page 87) or store-bought pound cake

1 Make and chill the pastry cream.

2 Set aside about 2 tablespoons of the preserves. Toss the remaining preserves and berries together in a medium bowl. Let stand 10 to 15 minutes. Taste the mix and add a little lemon juice and/or sugar if you think the berries need a little sweetness or acidity.

3 Beat the cream in a clean bowl until it holds soft peaks. Add the pastry cream to the bowl and fold into the whipped cream until only a few small streaks of white remain.

4 Build the trifle in a 2-quart/8-cup bowl. A glass bowl with straight sides is best. Scatter half the cake cubes over the bottom of the bowl. If your bowl has rounded sides and is wider at the top than the bottom, start with slightly less than half the cake. Leave enough space between the cake cubes for the berry juices to fill and soften the cake. Spoon about half the berry mixture over the cake (less berry mixture if you used less cake). Spoon half the cream over the berries and smooth the top of the cream into an even layer. As you build, keep an eye on the sides of the bowl. You should see some of each layer clearly through the sides of the bowl. Repeat with the remaining cake, berry mixture, and cream. Cover the trifle with plastic wrap and refrigerate for at least 4 hours and up to 1 day.

5 Remove the trifle from the refrigerator about half an hour before serving. Smooth the top of the cream layer and swirl the reserved 2 tablespoons preserves over the cream as decoration. Spoon the trifle into serving bowls. There is no neat way to do this—that is part of the appeal of a trifle.

Pastry Cream

The creamy deliciousness inside an éclair? Pastry cream. Between the layers of a napoleon? Pastry cream. The bottom layer of a fancy French fruit tart? You got it, pastry cream. Once you get the hang of very simple pastry cream, the dessert world is your oyster. Rose uses it for her Lingonberry Trifle.

MAKES: 1¾ CUPS • PREP TIME: 5 MINUTES • COOK TIME: 20 MINUTES

1½ cups whole milk

½ cup sugar

2 egg yolks

3 tablespoons cornstarch

½ teaspoon salt

4 tablespoons butter, cut into 6 pieces

1　Heat the milk and sugar to steaming over medium-low heat in a medium saucepan, stirring occasionally.

2　Meanwhile, whisk the yolks, cornstarch, and salt together in a medium bowl. Set the bowl on top of a damp kitchen towel to keep it steady and slowly pour in about ½ cup of the hot milk mixture, whisking constantly. Whisk the egg mix into the milk remaining in the saucepan and continue heating and stirring until the mixture is very thick and a bubble pops up here and there.

3　Scrape the pastry cream into the medium bowl and whisk in the butter pieces one by one. Transfer the pastry cream to a storage container, press a piece of plastic wrap directly to the surface to prevent a skin from forming, and refrigerate. The pastry cream may be kept refrigerated for up to 1 week.

"Yak Snacks"

Flenderheuven would be just another ho-hum bowl of oatmeal if not paired with Yak Snacks—delicious crackers made from yak intestines. It is regrettable, but understandable, that hardly anyone takes the time to make Yak Snacks from scratch anymore. Yak intestines can be hard to come by and the process of turning them into crispy crackers can be daunting. But what to do when flenderheuven is on the menu? Fortunately, for those of us who still crave them, there is a plant in Tyler's Landing that makes traditional Yak Snacks. Just don't buy a house downwind from it.

Maple Syrup-Honey-Brown Sugar-Molasses-Rice Krispies Log

Can there ever be too much of a good thing? For those who grew up preparing and sharing Maple Syrup-Honey-Brown Sugar-Molasses-Rice Krispies Log—St. Olaf's signature snack—a single log just won't cut it. Rose, gearing up for a visit from daughter Kristin and granddaughter/ aspiring astronaut-dater Charley, pulled out all the stops and prepares one of these super-sweet-and-sticky logs in honor of their visit. Kristin doubles down, bringing her own homemade MSHBSMRKLs as thank-you gifts for the rest of the girls.

By all accounts, MSHBSMRKL is an acquired taste, but not one Dorothy is likely to acquire any time soon.

Some people put flour in it, but I think it makes it too heavy. My kids liked it this way.

Tell me, Rose, do any of your kids still have their own teeth?

Kurflugenlugen

Take Dorothy's suggestion to cut corners using frozen Kurflugenlugen? Rose?? Never!

Kurflugenlugen, aka candied herring, must be made at home, especially when it is the centerpiece of an important meal—like a luncheon where you meet your boyfriend's daughter for the first time. Store-bought Kurflugenlugen could never strike the perfect balance of sweet and fishy flavor that made Rose's version the toast of St. Olaf. (Using Red Hots candy for the eyes is just one of Rose's special touches!) Carefully creating your own Kurflugenlugen is worth the effort just to watch people devour whole herring after herring, including the tail, but hopefully not before they've first made a wish!

As Miles said about Rose's homemade candied herring, "The herring was not only delicious, but it looked happy!" Try getting that out of a freezer case!

Minnesota Antifreeze

A mugful of this gets Rose's motor running on a chilly (?) Miami morning.

MAKES: 2 MUGS • PREP TIME: 5 MINUTES • COOK TIME: 5 MINUTES

⅓ cup evaporated milk

3 tablespoons unsweetened dark cocoa powder

2 to 3 tablespoons sugar

2 cups milk

Toppings (optional; pick a favorite): marshmallow cream, mini marshmallows, a dab of whipped cream

Bottomings (optional; add instead of or along with toppings): add a dab of chocolate spread or peanut butter to the bottom of the mug before pouring in the hot cocoa.

Whisk the evaporated milk, cocoa powder, and sugar together in a small heavy saucepan. Place over medium-low heat and whisk until the sugar and cocoa are blended into the evaporated milk. Pour in the milk in a thin steady stream and continue whisking until the milk is steaming and bubbles form around the edges of the saucepan. Pour into 2 hot mugs, with the toppings or bottomings of your choice.

Double Fudge Chocolate Cheesecake

If there's no problem that can't be solved with a little cheesecake, that must mean there's no international crisis that can't be solved with double fudge chocolate cheesecake!

MAKES: ONE 10-INCH CHEESECAKE (16 SLICES) • PREP TIME: 30 MINUTES • BAKE TIME: 1 HOUR 15 MINUTES —

FOR THE CRUST:

1 package (9 ounces) Nabisco Famous Chocolate Wafers

⅓ cup sugar

5 tablespoons (2½ ounces) melted butter, at room temperature

¼ teaspoon salt

MAKE THE CRUST:

1 First eat a few of the cookies. You know you will anyway. Then grind the cookies and sugar in a food processor until very fine, stopping once or twice to scrape the bottom and sides of the bowl. Add the butter and process until the mix is very moist and starts to stick to the sides of the bowl. Set 2 tablespoons of the crumb mixture aside and move the rest of the crumb mixture to a 10-inch nonstick springform pan. Using a flat-bottom glass wrapped with plastic wrap, make an even layer of crust across the bottom of the pan, working the crumbs outward toward the sides of the pan. Then, with the sides of the glass, press the crumbs about 1 inch up the sides of the pan. Place the cake pan on a baking sheet large enough to hold it comfortably and refrigerate.

2 While the crust is chilling, heat the oven to 350°F with an oven rack in the center position.

There is nothing worse than being wide awake and scared and by yourself.

Oh, yes, there is! Being wide awake and scared and by yourself without a double fudge chocolate cheesecake in the freezer.

FOR THE CHEESECAKE BATTER:

12 ounces bittersweet chocolate (60%), broken or chopped into small pieces

1 pound cream cheese, at room temperature

1⅓ cups sugar

2 tablespoons cornstarch

¼ teaspoon salt

4 eggs, at room temperature

1 teaspoon vanilla

MAKE THE BATTER AND BAKE THE CAKE:

3 Put the broken or chopped chocolate in a heatproof bowl. Choose a saucepan large enough to hold the bowl steady when the bowl is set on top. Pour about an inch of water into the saucepan and place the saucepan, with the bowl over the water, over medium-low heat. Melt, stirring every few minutes with a heatproof spatula, until completely smooth and shiny. Do not let the water under the bowl come to a boil. Remove the pan from the heat but leave the bowl of chocolate over the hot water to keep warm.

4 In the bowl of a stand mixer or in a bowl using a handheld electric mixer, beat the cream cheese, sugar, cornstarch, and the salt until creamy, about 3 minutes. Add the eggs one at a time, beating well after each, then beat in the vanilla. Scrape the melted chocolate into the mixer bowl and mix on low speed, scraping the sides and bottom of the bowl several times, until well blended.

5 Pour the batter into the crust and wiggle the pan to help the batter settle into an even layer. Sprinkle the top of the batter with the reserved crumb mix, making a border around the edges of the batter (or decorating however you'd like).

6 Put the cheesecake on the tray in the oven and lower the temperature to 300°F. Bake 40 minutes. Gently rotate the baking sheet. Continue baking 30 to 40 minutes, until the cake is set around the edges, and the center 3 inches or so jiggles only slightly when you gently move the cake pan back and forth. Crack the oven door, turn off the oven, and let the cake sit for about an hour.

7 Remove the cake from the oven and transfer the cake pan to a cooling rack. Cool completely. Refrigerate the cheesecake until firm, at least 3 hours. Bring to room temperature about 45 minutes before serving. The cheesecake can be stored in the refrigerator, tightly wrapped, for up to several days, or cut into pieces, securely wrapped, and frozen for up to 3 months.

Blanche

> Let me get the cheesecake and we'll talk. . . . (*gasps*) Oh my god!

> Blanche, what's wrong?

> Here we are in the middle of a crisis and there's no cheesecake!

Blanche may not have the culinary experience shared by Rose and Sophia, but there is plenty that gets her going (in the kitchen, that is).

Blanche appreciates a delicious, but decidedly lighter, soup or salad, like "Everything" Mango-Pineapple Salad or Quickie Gazpacho, for her everyday meals. But when it comes to special occasions, that's when Blanche's fierce Southern pride kicks into high gear. Reflecting on her Georgia youth gets her worked up to make dishes like Corny Corn Bread, Pecan Pie, and Quick Hoppin' John that are are suitable for a crowd. Blanche's legendary fried chicken is just the ticket when she is cooking for a small group, like the rest of the Golden Girls.

She also sometimes cooks for just herself, and perhaps a gentleman caller who could use a little boost in the morning. A couple of fried eggs and a side of Country Ham with Red-Eye Gravy takes about five minutes from skillet to table, leaving plenty of time to clean up before Sophia wanders in and starts asking questions.

But suppose, just suppose, the Hunka-Hunka Burning Love Fan Club (the only unauthorized Elvis fan club in greater Miami) should hold a meeting at your house. . . . Don't fuss too much, just whip up a batch of Deviled Eggs and some Shrimp?! with one, two, or three dipping sauces and you're all set. Oh, and make a pitcher of Sloe Gin Fizzes and pass it round! It can't hurt.

Room for dessert? How about a dense Miami-influenced Orange Upside-Down Cake or a boozy Mint Julep Ice Cream? Blanche will be happy to join you—on the front porch swing, of course. If it brings you pleasure, Blanche says go for it.

"Everything" Mango-Pineapple Salad

With its scattering of seeds, this juicy salad looks a little like an everything bagel. It tastes a little like one, too, minus the garlic and onion. If you are buying pineapple already cut up—and why not?—there will likely be enough pineapple juice in the container to use in this salad. If not, supplement with or substitute orange juice. The cashews put this over the top, but they might not be your thing.

MAKES: 4 SERVINGS • PREP TIME: 10 MINUTES

2 tablespoons sesame seeds

1 tablespoon poppy seeds

1 cup yogurt

3 tablespoons pineapple and/or orange juice

2 tablespoons honey

Pinch of salt

2 cups diced (about ¾ inch) pineapple

1 ripe mango

¼ cup salted roasted cashews, coarsely crushed, optional

1 Toast the sesame seeds in a small skillet over low heat, tossing or shaking the pan constantly, until they are a light golden brown. Remove the pan from the heat and stir in the poppy seeds. Let cool.

2 Stir the yogurt, juice, honey, salt, and 1 tablespoon of the seed mix together in a medium bowl. Add the pineapple and toss to coat.

3 Slice along both flat sides of the mango pit to remove the fruit. With the skin still on, cut the mango into ½-inch wedges. Slip the knife between skin and fruit to peel the wedges. Slice the remaining fruit away from the sides of the pit, then peel it. Chop this "side fruit" coarsely and place in the center of a serving dish. Arrange the nicely cut and peeled mango wedges around the edges of the plate.

4 Spoon the pineapple and yogurt over the mango on the plate, letting the yogurt drip down onto the plate. Scatter the toasted seeds and cashews, if using, over the fruit and yogurt and serve.

GOLDEN WISDOM

Toasting the poppy seeds along with the sesame seeds would make them bitter. Warming them gently, as Blanche does here, brings out their flavor.

Country Ham with Red-Eye Gravy

With its bitter-strong flavor, a little Red-Eye Gravy goes a long way. And Blanche has another bit of wisdom when it comes to red-eye: If you haven't ever tried or made the gravy, it will make no sense at all to you on its own. On top of a salty/sweet/smoky slice of ham, however, it will make all the sense in the world.

MAKES: 4 SERVINGS • PREP TIME: 2 MINUTES (IF YOU ALREADY HAVE THE COFFEE BREWED) • COOK TIME: 15 MINUTES

2 tablespoons unsalted butter

12 thin slices of smoked country ham (about ½ pound)

½ cup hot brewed coffee

Fine sea or kosher salt and freshly ground black pepper

1 Heat about ½ tablespoon butter in a large heavy skillet over medium heat. When the butter is foaming, add half the ham slices. It's okay if they overlap a bit; they will shrink as they cook. Fry until they are lightly browned, about 3 minutes, then flip and brown the second side. Remove the ham to plates or a platter, add another ½ tablespoon butter to the pan, and repeat with the remaining ham.

2 Increase the heat to high for a minute, then pour in the hot coffee and bring to a boil. Continue boiling, scraping the bottom of the pan, until reduced by half, then remove from the heat. Add the remaining butter and swirl it into the sauce. Add salt and pepper to taste. Spoon a little—about a tablespoon per portion—over the ham.

Blanche, try to remember . . . gravy isn't a beverage.

Quickie Gazpacho

Sometimes there doesn't seem to be enough time in a day to take a full-fledged break to do something nice for you and a friend. That's when it's time to slip in a quickie. We're talking about gazpacho, of course, and fifteen minutes is about all you need to whip up a batch of cooling soup bursting with fresh flavor. Serve it right out of the blender or take an hour or so to chill it. In either case, make two batches and serve it in coffee cups at your next summer fiesta.

MAKES: 4 CUPS OR 4 TO 6 SERVINGS • PREP TIME: 15 MINUTES • CHILL TIME (IF YOU LIKE): 1 HOUR

1 pound ripe tomatoes

1 large or 3 small (Kirby or minis) cucumbers

1 red or yellow bell pepper

½ small red onion

¼ cup coarsely chopped fresh basil

2 tablespoons olive oil, the fruitier the better, plus more for drizzling

1 tablespoon red wine vinegar

1 jalapeño, cored, seeded, and minced (optional)

1½ teaspoons fine sea or kosher salt

Salad Croutons (page 159)

1 Prep the vegetables, adding them to a medium bowl as you go: Core the tomatoes, and cut them into 1-inch chunks. Trim the cucumbers, and cut them in half and then into 1-inch lengths. Remove the stem and seeds from the pepper, and cut the pepper into 1-inch chunks. Cut the onion into 1-inch chunks.

2 Add the olive oil, vinegar, and jalapeño, if using, to the bowl. Toss well and let stand 5 minutes.

3 Blend in batches at low speed until coarsely pureed (or finely chopped, depending on how you look at it). You should be able to see small bits of all the vegetables. Serve at room temperature or chilled with a drizzle of olive oil and croutons. If you do chill, remember that this gazpacho is best eaten within 2 days.

Cheesy Grits Casserole

These are some fine grits! A firm top layer, topped with golden brown cheddar, reveals a center of creamy, cheesy, perfectly cooked grits.

MAKES: 6 TO 8 SERVINGS • PREP TIME: 10 MINUTES • COOK TIME: 1 HOUR

1 cup coarse yellow grits

¾ teaspoon salt

3 tablespoons unsalted butter, plus more for the baking dish

2 eggs

½ cup milk

Few dashes Tabasco-brand hot sauce or other hot sauce

Several grinds black pepper

2½ cups sharp cheddar cheese

⅓ cup grated Parmesan cheese, optional

1 Stir together the grits, 3 cups cold water, and the salt in a heavy 2-quart saucepan. Place over medium-low heat and bring to a boil. Adjust the heat so just one or two bubbles come to the surface at a time. Stir until the grits are thick and mound slightly on a spoon, about 10 minutes. Continue stirring, paying attention to the bottom and sides of the pan, until the grits are tender, about 10 minutes more. If the grits thicken up more before they become tender, add water, 1 to 2 tablespoons at a time, to loosen them up a little.

2 While the grits are cooking, heat the oven to 350°F with a rack in the upper third position. Butter an 8-inch square baking dish or other 6-cup baking dish.

3 Scrape the grits into a bowl and stir in 3 tablespoons butter. Let the grits cool a little while you whisk together the eggs, milk, hot sauce, and black pepper in a small bowl. Beat the egg mixture, then 2 cups of the cheddar and Parmesan cheese, into the grits.

4 Scrape the grits mixture into the prepared dish, then sprinkle the remaining ½ cup cheddar and the Parmesan, if using, over the top. Bake until the top is golden brown and the casserole is firm when poked but with some give, about 40 minutes. Let stand 5 to 10 minutes before serving.

Shrimp?!
(A Simple Guide to the Best Shrimp Cocktail, as Almost Served to Dr. Jonathan Newman)

Blanche prides herself on being the quintessential Southern hostess. But when Dr. Jonathan Newman visited, she couldn't stop saying the wrong thing. Even Blanche's perfectly cooked shrimp couldn't save the day.

MAKES: 4 SERVINGS • PREP TIME: 15 MINUTES • COOK TIME: A FEW MINUTES, MAX

8 cups water

1 lemon, cut into thick slices

1 tablespoon salt

2 bay leaves

1 pound shrimp in the shell, the larger the better (see notes)

FOR THE PERFECTLY COOKED SHRIMP:

1 Heat the water, lemon, salt, and bay leaves to a boil in a large saucepan.

2 Meanwhile, peel the shrimp, leaving the tail shell in place if you like. Make a shallow cut along the back of the shrimp. Remove the vein and grit, and wipe along the cut to make sure to remove everything.

3 Turn off the heat under the water. Slip the shrimp into the hot water. Let stand until the shrimp are pink and cooked through: 3 to 4 minutes for U15s (see notes) and 2 to 3 minutes for 21/25s. Drain immediately and spread out on a baking sheet to cool. The shrimp may be eaten at room temperature or refrigerated for up to 1 day and served chilled.

Notes: Yes, shrimp are sold already shelled and deveined, and you can use those for this recipe if you like. But it's easier to tell the freshness status of shell-on shrimp. Shells on shrimp should feel firm, be brightly colored (whatever the color is), and smell delicious.

Regardless of which spectacular name may be given to shrimp at your fish shop or grocery—Jumbo, Super Colossal, or Really, Really Big—the only true way to tell a shrimp's size is by the numbers. If there is a range given, such as 21/25, there will be between 21 and 25 shrimp per pound. Of course, a 21/25 shrimp will be bigger than a 26/30. If there is a U in the description, as in U15, that means there are under 15 shrimp per pound. It's really quite simple, and more and more places are selling shrimp according to this system.

FOR THE DIPPING SAUCE(S), ANY OR ALL:

Avocado Puree

MAKES: 1 CUP • PREP TIME: 10 MINUTES

1 ripe but firm medium
Hass avocado

Juice of 1 small lime, or as needed

3 tablespoons olive oil

Fine sea or kosher salt and freshly
ground black pepper

Remove the peel and pit from the avocado. Cut the flesh into cubes and toss together with the lime juice in a small bowl. Whisk the avocado, adding the olive oil bit by bit until the oil is incorporated and the sauce is left slightly chunky. If you like a silky-smooth sauce, puree the avocado, lime juice, and oil in a food processor, adding the oil slowly while the motor is running. In either case, season to taste with salt, freshly ground pepper, and additional lime juice if necessary. The sauce may be made up to several hours in advance. Refrigerate with plastic wrap pressed directly onto the surface to prevent it from turning brown.

Classic Cocktail Sauce

MAKES: 1 CUP • PREP TIME: 10 MINUTES

1 cup bottled chili sauce (Heinz makes one that is perfect for cocktail sauce) or ketchup

1 tablespoon lemon juice

2 to 3 teaspoons bottled horseradish, including some of the liquid in the jar

1 teaspoon hot sauce, or to taste (know thy crowd!)

1 teaspoon Worcestershire sauce

Whisk all ingredients together in a small bowl. Cover with plastic and refrigerate until needed. Will keep for up to a week.

Tex-Mex Grainy-Maynie

MAKES: 1 CUP • PREP TIME: 5 MINUTES

½ cup grainy mustard

½ cup mayonnaise

3 tablespoons chopped cilantro

1 tablespoon finely chopped bottled jalapeño peppers or pepperoncinis

Whisk all ingredients together in a small bowl. Cover and refrigerate until needed. Will keep for up to a week.

Deviled Eggs

About the same time Blanche started chasing Ham Lushbough around, her mama took her aside and taught her the fine Southern art of making deviled eggs. No picnic or summer get-together is truly a party until these deviled eggs make their appearance.

MAKES: 12 • PREP TIME: 35 MINUTES • COOK TIME: 11 MINUTES

6 eggs

3 tablespoons mayonnaise or Miracle Whip dressing

2 teaspoons Dijon mustard

½ teaspoon dry mustard (if you don't have dry mustard, up the Dijon a little)

1 teaspoon lemon juice

½ teaspoon Tabasco-brand hot sauce, or a little more

½ teaspoon Worcestershire sauce

Fine sea or kosher salt and freshly ground black pepper

1 Put the eggs in a saucepan that they fit into in a single layer. Pour enough water over them to cover by an inch. Heat to boiling, reduce the heat to very low, and cook without boiling 11 minutes. Drain the water and submerge the eggs in ice water for about 10 minutes.

2 Take the eggs out one by one and roll them on the countertop until they're cracked on all sides. Tap the ends to crack those for good measure. Put them back in the water and let them sit for half an hour.

3 Peel the eggs and cut them in half. Scoop the yolks into a small bowl. Line the whites up on a quarter sheet pan or big dish lined with damp paper towels to keep them from sliding around.

4 Add the mayonnaise, Dijon and ground mustards, lemon juice, Tabasco, and Worcestershire to the yolks and beat them (a hand mixer works nicely) until very smooth. Season to taste with salt and pepper. Scoop the filling into a pastry bag fitted with a star tip (or a sandwich bag with a cut corner) and pipe the filling into the eggs. Or else just spoon the filling into the eggs. Deviled eggs go so quickly, it's not like anyone is going to be able to admire your piping prowess anyway. Serve as is or "dress up the devil" (opposite).

— GOLDEN WISDOM —

Half sheet pans (18 x 13 inch) and quarter sheet pans (13 x 9 inch) are available at restaurant supply stores and housewares stores. Look for heavy, not flimsy.

What's the Ham short for, Ham?

My guess is Ham and Potatoes.

DRESSING UP THE DEVIL

Dorothy would probably choose a functional and easy way to decorate the finished eggs. Let's say a nice sprig of dill and a diamond shape of bottled pimiento. All the eggs would get the same topping and then be arranged in an orderly fashion on a tray.

Rose, of course, would know of someone back in St. Olaf who decorated his deviled eggs with an assortment of toppings: the ever-present herring, M&M's candies, julienne of banana, another deviled egg, and so on. Beware if Rose invites you over for a nosh!

Sophia would most likely say, "Screw it. Just put them out there. I got a bingo match to get to!"

Now, Blanche, on the other hand, might bring all her appreciation of the fine arts to bear and turn the platter into a canvas. Working from a palette of ingredients—julienne of roasted red peppers, thinly sliced chives, pitted black olives cut into circles, slivers of anchovy, crumbled crisp bacon, and dill sprigs, for example—she would make each deviled egg a unique mini masterpiece and arrange them on small, unique plates to be scattered throughout the room.

Blanche Devereaux Fries Some Chicken

Every once in a while, Blanche Elizabeth (or Marie, depending who you ask) Devereaux (née Hollingsworth) forgoes the company of a man and whips up a batch of fried chicken for herself and the girls. Blanche's fried chicken takes some patience, like making a beautiful handmade patchwork quilt, or so Blanche has heard from people who go in for such things.

There are three steps to B.E.D.'s perfect fried chicken. First, a soak in salted, slightly spicy buttermilk that doubles as a brine and yields beautifully seasoned, tender, and moist chicken. Second, a thorough but light coating of flour and, third, a nice slow bath in hot fat. Read through this recipe, including the notes, a few times before you start. It really is very simple, but familiarity with the steps can't hurt. Last but not least, if you haven't invested a few bucks in an instant-read thermometer, this is the time to do it.

MAKES: 4 SERVINGS • PREP TIME: 30 MINUTES, PLUS 1 TO 2 DAYS MARINATING TIME • COOK TIME: 35 MINUTES

2 cups buttermilk, at room temperature

3 to 4 tablespoons kosher salt

1 tablespoon sugar

½ teaspoon cayenne pepper

One 3¼-pound chicken, cut into 10 parts (2 wings, 2 thighs, 2 drumsticks, and 4 breast pieces; see notes)

All-purpose flour

Vegetable oil or solid vegetable shortening

——GOLDEN WISDOM——

Lay the chicken pieces away from you so any splatters go toward the back of the pan and not onto you.

DAY ONE:

1 Stir the buttermilk, salt, sugar, and cayenne together in a medium bowl. Pat the chicken dry, add it to the marinade, and toss it well to coat the pieces completely. Cover and refrigerate for at least 1 day and up to 2 days. Turn the pieces in the marinade when you think of it.

2 That's it for day one. Once the chicken is marinating, you're free to call Mel Bushman, the Zipper King, for a night out.

DAY TWO:

1 Pick the chicken pieces out of the brine and place on a baking sheet. Don't worry if they're still dripping with marinade. Separate into like pieces—wings, drumsticks, thighs, and breast pieces. Set a baking sheet with a thick layer of all-purpose flour next to that, and a cooling rack set over another baking sheet (or sheet of parchment paper or paper towels) next to that.

2 Work with the drumsticks and thighs one by one: Smooth out the skin to cover the chicken and tap each piece against the side of the baking sheet so only a thin layer of the buttermilk remains. Move the drumsticks and thighs into the flour as you finish with them. Wash and dry your hands.

3 Toss the chicken pieces around to coat them well, then bounce them from hand to hand to get rid of extra flour (which would fall off the chicken, burn in the oil, and lend a burned flavor to the chicken). Move them onto the wire cooling rack to set the coating. Wash your hands again; they'll need it.

4 Fill a large heavy frying pan one-third full of oil or shortening. Heat the fat over medium heat to 300°F. If you don't have a deep-frying thermometer, use this test: the tip of a coated drumstick will give off a quick, steady stream of bubbles when held in the oil for a few seconds. Carefully lay the chicken pieces skin side down in the pan.

5 Now comes the important part: regulating the heat. Adjust the heat until there is a nice steady sizzle. The heat shouldn't be so high that the chicken is spattering and spitting or so low that it's just lying there like one of Blanche's bad dates. Once it's in, leave the chicken be so it forms a nice crust on the bottom and won't stick when turned. If you move the chicken too soon, some of the coating will stick to the pan, which, like the stray flour mentioned above, will burn and change the flavor of the chicken.

6 While the drumsticks and thighs are frying, pass the baking sheet of coating flour through a sieve to remove lumps, flour the wings and breast pieces, and move them to the rack. By then, the drumsticks will have a nice golden-brown color on the underside and will be ready to turn. Turn and continue frying, paying attention to the heat, until an instant-read thermometer inserted into the thickest part of the drumsticks and thighs away from the bone reads 165°F or above. You'll also notice that juices will run out of the places where you poke with the thermometer. Those juices should be clear, not pink. Test in a few places.

7 Drain the drumsticks and thighs on paper towels or on a sturdy brown paper bag. Very carefully, strain the oil into a pot and wipe out the skillet with a big wad of paper towels (use oven mitts to hold the paper towels). Strain the oil, again very carefully, back into the pan(s) and start all over again with the wings and breast pieces. Serve the chicken at room temperature, which is a wonderful thing.

Notes: Discover a hidden resource: your supermarket butchers. If you cannot find a chicken cut into 10 pieces in the supermarket case, ask the people in the butcher department. You'll be surprised how happy most of them are to help. You might even ask them to cut up a chicken of your choice for you. Pick out a nice free-range, kosher, or organic chicken and give it a shot.

If this is your first time doing serious panfrying, stick to the one skillet. If you're a little more familiar with the process, set two heavy skillets up with fat, coat all the chicken pieces at once, and fry the thighs and drumsticks in one and the wings and breast pieces in the other.

Moving on to your brown belt in chicken frying, fry two chickens for a larger crowd: Use two pans and fry all the drumsticks and thighs in the first round and all the wings and breast pieces in the second.

Southern Not-Fried Chicken

Blanche looooves her fried chicken, but she knows that too much of a good thing would make it hard to get into her slim-fit dresses for nickel beer night at the Rusty Anchor. Here's her solution to the problem of a fried chicken craving—a crunchy-coated "fried" chicken made without chicken skin or scads of frying oil.

MAKES: 4 SERVINGS • PREP TIME: 15 MINUTES, PLUS 3+ HOURS MARINATING • COOK TIME: 30 MINUTES

4 large bone-in chicken thighs (see note), about 2 pounds

1½ cups buttermilk

6 good dashes hot sauce (Frank's brand works well)

1½ teaspoons fine sea salt

1 egg

1 cup Toasted Panko (page 32)

1 teaspoon onion powder

Vegetable oil (or olive oil) cooking spray

Note: Chicken thighs run in all sizes. For this recipe, choose bone-in chicken thighs that weigh about 8 ounces each (a 2-pound package for 4 thighs). This larger size and the bone means the chicken will take longer to cook— good news for a crisp coating. Bone-in chicken thighs are almost always sold with the skin on. The skin can be easily removed.

1 Pull the skin off the chicken thighs, if necessary, and trim off any fat. Stir the buttermilk, hot sauce, and salt together in a medium bowl. Roll the chicken thighs in the seasoned buttermilk, cover the bowl, and refrigerate at least 3 hours and up to a day. Turn the chicken thighs in the buttermilk marinade when you think about it.

2 Make a production line: Set a cooling rack over a baking sheet, and place it next to you on the counter. Beat the egg and a tablespoon or so of water together in a shallow bowl until very well blended. Stir the Toasted Panko and onion powder together in a second shallow bowl or on a plate, and spread the mix out. Remove a thigh from the buttermilk and shake it gently to remove most of the buttermilk. Turn the thigh in the egg until completely coated, hold it over the bowl for a few seconds to let extra egg drip off, and then lay it in the bread crumbs. Turn the thigh in the crumbs and pat the crumbs gently to help them stick. Turn and pat once more on each side. Set the coated thigh on the rack and continue with the rest of the chicken. Let stand 20 minutes.

3 Meanwhile, heat the oven to 475°F with a rack in the center position. When ready to cook, remove the cooling rack from the baking pan, line the pan with parchment paper or aluminum foil, and spray with nonstick cooking spray. Arrange the chicken pieces on the foil with some room between them. Bake until the chicken is golden brown and reads 165°F on an instant-read thermometer at the thickest part away from a bone (or the juices run clear, not pink, when poked with a skewer), about 35 minutes. Let rest 5 to 10 minutes before serving. Delicious at room temperature, too.

Avocado-Dill-Yogurt Dressing

MAKES: 1¼ CUPS • PREP TIME: 15 MINUTES

½ avocado, pitted and peeled

½ cup loosely packed dill leaves and stems

⅓ cup plain yogurt

2 tablespoons lemon juice

½ teaspoon fine sea salt

½ cup olive oil

Several grinds black pepper

1 Put the avocado, dill, yogurt, lemon juice, and salt in a blender and blend until the dill is finely chopped. Add 1 tablespoon water and blend until smooth. With the motor running, drizzle in the olive oil. Stop about halfway through and add a little water if the blender needs help. Scrape down the sides of the blender jar a few times with a rubber spatula. Drizzle in the rest of the oil and more water if you need it to make a smooth, creamy dressing. Season with pepper.

2 Scrape the dressing into a small storage container, preferably glass. Press a piece of plastic wrap directly to the surface and cover the container. Store no more than 2 days.

GOLDEN WISDOM

Marguerite, the girls' housekeeper, left in a huff. She didn't even share her aphrodisiac recipe with Blanche, or her secret for keeping avocados bright green with the rest of the girls. So the girls used a little science instead: Use the acid from citrus juice and/or yogurt to keep avocado bright green. And keep air away from the dressing or guac by storing it with a piece of plastic wrap pressed directly on the surface.

ROYAL VEGETABLE PLATE, WITHOUT THE ROYAL

Blanche is always on the lookout for tasty ways to keep her figure! With all the time she spends tracking down miracle low-calorie salad dressings, she could make batch after batch of her own to keep on hand. These two dressings are quick to whip up, delicious, and last at least a couple of days in the fridge. All you need is a healthy mix of greens and vegetables and fruits to pair them with.

None of this has to take the time and effort Blanche puts into her Royal Vegetable Plate. Keep on hand lots of greens, vegetables, and mix-ins, as well as either the Avocado-Dill-Yogurt Dressing or the Citrus 1-2-3 Dressing, and you're in business. (See Dorothy's Guide to Packing a Workday Lunch on page 14 for a slew of ideas.)

1-2-3 Citrus Dressing

Why rely on bottled low-cal dressing with all the flavor of tap water? This dressing is called 1-2-3 for the amounts of the citrus juices used to make it but also for its ease. Pair it with fruit salad, avocado slices, steamed or grilled seafood, grilled chicken, and, of course, greens.

MAKES: ABOUT 1 CUP • PREP TIME: 10 MINUTES ————————————

1 tablespoon lemon juice

2 tablespoons lime juice

3 tablespoons orange juice

About ½ cup fruity olive oil

Fine sea or kosher salt and freshly ground black pepper

12 chives, cut diagonally into 1-inch lengths

Combine all ingredients except the chives in a 2-cup (or so) jar with a tight-fitting lid. Shake very well. Leave at room temperature for up to 4 hours or refrigerate for up to a day. Bring refrigerated dressing to full room temperature before serving. Just before serving, add the chives, shake again, and check for salt and pepper.

It's called creamy zesty Italian. Only has one calorie. What do you think?

If you ran it under the faucet, it would have more flavor.

Shoot.

Honey, beware anybody who says "no calories," "absolutely no charge," and "let's just go lie down in bed and watch TV."

"Orange Duck" for Two

Although duck à l'orange is one of Blanche's favorite dishes, it's hard to imagine her having the patience to see this all the way through. Maybe one of her many gentleman admirers—Jake from VIP Catering?—can lend a hand.

MAKES: 2 GENEROUS SERVINGS • PREP TIME: 10 MINUTES , PLUS 4+ HOURS CHILL TIME • COOK TIME: 50 MINUTES

1 whole (i.e., double) duck breast, also known as magret de canard, about 1¼ pounds

2 teaspoons coarse sea or kosher salt

½ teaspoon ground black pepper

¼ teaspoon ground clove

2 cups store-bought, low-sodium chicken broth or Rotisserie Chicken Broth (page 71)

¼ cup orange juice

1 orange

1 If necessary, cut the duck breast into 2 individual breasts. Turn them skin side down and trim any skin and fat that extends beyond the meat. With a very sharp knife, score the skin side at 1-inch intervals, going through the fat but not into the meat. Pat the duck breasts very dry with paper towels.

2 Stir the salt, pepper, and cloves together in a small bowl. Season both sides of the duck breasts generously with the mix. To ensure a crisp skin, put the duck breasts skin side up on a large plate and refrigerate, uncovered, for at least 4 hours and up to overnight. (Hint: overnight is better.)

3 Bring the duck to room temperature an hour before cooking. Meanwhile, grate ½ teaspoon zest from the orange and set it aside. With a vegetable peeler, remove two 1-inch-wide strips of zest from the rest of the orange, removing as little of the white pith in place as possible. Bring the stock, orange juice, and the two wide strips of orange zest to a boil in a small saucepan. Boil until the glaze is reduced to ½ cup and is lightly thickened. Set aside in the saucepan.

4 Put the duck breast skin side down in a heavy skillet (cast iron works well) and set the skillet over very low heat. Render the fat from the skin of the duck breast until the skin is deep brown and only a thin layer of fat remains. This may take up to 30 minutes. Be patient and don't turn up the heat. The idea is to crisp the skin and render as much fat as possible without burning the skin.

Dirk

When I'm with you, I kind of feel like I'm home . . . with Mom.

Waiter! Eighty-six the watercress. I'll have the orange duck and a double Jack Daniel's on the rocks.

5 Flip the duck and raise the heat to medium. Cook until the internal temperature reaches 130°F to 135°F at the thickest part for a medium-rare duck breast. (See page 29 for info on instant-read thermometers.) Cook longer—to an internal temperature of 145°F to 150°F—for a medium duck breast. Remove the duck breast to a cutting board, skin side up, and let rest 10 minutes.

6 Meanwhile, remove the pan from the heat, drain off as much fat as possible, and pour the orange juice reduction into the pan. Scrape with a rubber spatula to remove the crunchies from the bottom of the pan.

7 Using a very sharp knife, cut the duck into ½-inch slices on an angle. Arrange the slices overlapping on a plate and pour the sauce around the slices. Serve immediately.

Quick Hoppin' John

There is no wrong way to make or serve Hoppin' John. Blanche's father, Big Daddy, likes his with rice stirred into the beans for a stewy Hoppin' John. Her sister Virginia spoons her rice onto one side of the bowl and the beans alongside the rice. Her other sister, Charmaine, ladles her beans right on top of her rice. And Blanche . . . well, she favors whatever makes Big Daddy happy.

MAKES: 6 CUPS OR 4 TO 6 SERVINGS • PREP TIME: 15 MINUTES • COOK TIME: 30 MINUTES (SOME UNATTENDED)

3 tablespoons butter

2½ cups diced smoked ham (about 8 ounces)

2 celery stalks, trimmed and diced fine

1 large yellow onion, diced fine

1 small red bell pepper, cored, seeded, and diced fine

2 cloves garlic, minced

Fine sea or kosher salt

Two 15-ounce cans black-eyed peas, drained and rinsed

2½ cups Rotisserie Chicken Broth (page 71) or store-bought chicken broth

¼ to ½ teaspoon cayenne pepper

Cooked rice

1   Heat the butter in a heavy medium casserole dish over medium-low heat until foaming. Add the ham and cook, stirring, until lightly browned, about 5 minutes. Stir in the celery, onion, red pepper, and garlic. Season lightly with salt and cook, stirring occasionally, until the vegetables are softened, about 5 minutes.

2   Add the peas, chicken broth, and cayenne. Bring to a boil, then adjust the heat so the broth is simmering. Cook, stirring occasionally, 15 minutes. If time allows, let the Hoppin' John sit off the heat for an hour or two before reheating to serve.

3   About 20 minutes before serving, make the rice. While the rice is cooking, reheat the Hoppin' John over low heat if necessary.

4   Serve the rice and beans stirred together, side by side or one atop the other. Excellent with Corny Corn Bread (page 129).

Honey-Bourbon-Glazed Carrots

Maybe Blanche got the idea for this simple side dish from the bottle of whiskey inside Big Daddy's Bible. Whatever the inspiration, the combination of honey and bourbon is right at home with glazed carrots.

MAKES: ABOUT 3½ CUPS OR 4 SERVINGS • PREP TIME: 15 MINUTES • COOK TIME: 20 MINUTES

1 pound carrots

1 tablespoon unsalted butter

Fine sea or kosher salt

2 teaspoons bourbon

1 tablespoon honey

Freshly ground black pepper

1 Peel and trim the carrots. Cut them crosswise and on an angle into ½- to 1-inch lengths—1 inch starting at the thin end and tapering down to ½ inch near the thick end.

2 Heat the carrots, butter, a large pinch of salt, and ½ cup water to boiling in a deep 9- to 10-inch skillet over medium heat. Cover and boil 5 minutes.

3 Uncover, add the bourbon and honey, and continue cooking until the carrots are slightly tender and the liquid is almost gone. (If the carrots aren't tender enough for your liking when the liquid is cooked off, add and cook off water, 2 tablespoons at a time, untill they are.) Reduce the heat to low and continue cooking until all the liquid is gone and the carrots are tender, but not mushy, and begin to brown in the remaining butter, about 6 minutes. Season with salt, if necessary, and pepper. Serve hot.

Golden Beets, Atlanta Style

MAKES: 4 SERVINGS • PREP TIME: 15 MINUTES • COOK TIME: 1½ HOURS (MOSTLY UNATTENDED)

1½ pounds golden beets

2 tablespoons plain yogurt

1 tablespoon white wine vinegar or lemon juice

1 tablespoon thinly sliced chives

½ teaspoon sugar or honey

Fine sea or kosher salt and freshly ground black pepper

1 Heat the oven to 400°F. Line a baking sheet with aluminum foil.

2 Scrub the beets, but leave them unpeeled. Put them on the baking sheet and bake until tender when poked with a paring knife, about 1½ hours. The cooking time for beets may vary quite a bit, so start testing after an hour.

3 While the beets are baking, stir the yogurt, vinegar, chives, and sugar together in a medium bowl.

4 Remove the beets and cool until you can handle them—the warmer they are, the easier they will be to peel and the more flavor from the dressing they will absorb. Peel the beets, simply pulling off the skin when possible and scraping off the skin in the places where it sticks.

5 Cut the beets into wedges and toss with the dressing. Add salt and pepper to taste. The beets may be kept at room temperature for up to several hours. If possible, avoid refrigerating the beets. If you do, bring them up to room temperature and check the seasonings before serving.

DON'T LET SOPHIA CATCH YOU THROWING AWAY THOSE BEET GREENS!

Search out beets that have bright green bushy leaves. The greens are a treat unto themselves. Cut the leaves from the stems. Wash and cut up the greens, and toss them into a panful of any sautéed greens, like the collards on page 125. Or use them in this simple dinner for two: Wash and spin-dry the beet greens, then cut them into ½-inch ribbons. Heat a large pot of salted water to boiling. In the meantime, heat a good glug of olive oil in a large sauté pan. Slice 2 cloves of garlic and add them to the oil along with a large pinch of crushed red pepper and, if you like, 3 or 4 anchovy fillets. When the garlic is lightly browned and the anchovy fillets are falling apart, add the beet greens and cook, stirring just until wilted. Pull the pan from the heat. Stir 4 ounces of spaghetti or linguine into the boiling water and cook, stirring, until al dente. Spoon about ½ cup of the pasta cooking water into the sauté pan and drain the pasta. Add the pasta to the beet greens and heat over medium-low, teasing the beet greens apart with a fork, until there is just enough of the sauce to lightly coat the spaghetti. Season with salt if necessary and serve with grated pecorino Romano or Parmesan cheese.

Naughty Blanche Collard Greens

You just never know what kind of mood Blanche is going to be in, especially during "the change." Here's a recipe for collards that fits Naughty Blanche's mood.

MAKES: 2 CUPS/4 SERVINGS • PREP TIME: 15 MINUTES • COOK TIME: 15 TO 20 MINUTES

1½ pounds collard greens, preferably with smaller, thinner leaves

4 slices bacon

2 cloves garlic, sliced thin

¼ teaspoon crushed red pepper flakes

1 to 2 teaspoons sugar

Fine sea or kosher salt

Note: If you want a healthier option, aka "Good Blanche Collard Greens," prep the greens the same way but skip the bacon and go to step 4, cooking them in 1 tablespoon vegetable oil instead of fat. Replace sugar with ¼ cup orange juice.

1 Fill a large bowl with water or clean your sink well and fill that with cool water. Remove the stems and leaf veins from the leaves. Either pull them out slowly starting at the thick stem end or cut them out with a paring knife. This is a quick-cooking collards recipe, so you'll want to trim as much of the stem/leaf vein as you can.

2 Cut the leaves in half lengthwise. Stack up several halves and cut them crosswise into ½-inch strips. Swish the leaves around in the water to clean them thoroughly. Let them sit several minutes so the dirt settles to the bottom, then lift the leaves into a salad spinner. Spin dry. The collards can be prepared this far up to a day in advance. Wrap them loosely in paper towels, put them in a plastic bag, and refrigerate until needed.

3 Put the bacon slices in a large, heavy skillet, and set the skillet over medium-low heat. Cook, turning once or twice, until browned and crisp, about 8 minutes. Remove to a plate and set aside.

4 Add the garlic and hot pepper to the fat in the pan and let sizzle just until the garlic starts to turn brown around the edges, about 2 minutes. Add a big handful of collards. Stir until wilted and bright green, about 2 minutes. Keep adding collards as the previous batch wilts until all the collards are in the pan. Sprinkle the sugar over the collards and add 2 tablespoons water. Cook and stir until all the water is gone and the collards are shiny with bacon fat and tender, but with some bite, about 4 minutes. Season with salt and transfer to a serving bowl. Crumble the bacon over the top.

Panfried Okra

If you like the unique, green flavor of okra but aren't a fan of its, ahem, unique texture, try this: simply season and coat the okra before flash-frying it. A favorite of Big Daddy's. For two people, this recipe can be a side dish, and for four it's a nibble with drinks.

MAKES: ABOUT ⅔ CUP • PREP TIME: 5 MINUTES • COOK TIME: 10 MINUTES

6 to 8 large okra pods

¼ teaspoon fine salt

Several grinds black pepper

3 tablespoons all-purpose flour

3 tablespoons fine yellow cornmeal

Vegetable oil

1 Top and tail the okra. Cut the pods on a slight angle into ¼-inch slices. There will be about 1 cup. Toss them together with the salt and pepper in a small bowl. Let stand for a minute or two, just until the okra becomes dewy.

2 Meanwhile, stir together the flour and cornmeal in a wide shallow dish. Pour enough oil into a wide heavy pan—cast iron is ideal—to fill ½ inch. Heat over medium-low heat.

3 Toss the okra with the cornmeal-flour coating until the okra is well coated. Bounce the okra in a sieve or back and forth between your hands to get rid of excess coating. Spread the okra out on a plate. In a few minutes, the coating on the okra will become very slightly moist; this is the time to fry! Check the oil; it is ready when a slice of okra slipped into the oil gives off a lively sizzle. Slip about half the okra slices into the oil and fry them, turning once (a slotted spoon works well), just until they are light golden brown; 2 to 3 minutes should do it. Don't overcook, or the okra will shrivel and the salt will be intensified. When the okra is done frying, it should be about the same size and shape it was when it went in the oil. If it starts to curl and shrink, you've gone too far. Drain on paper towels and serve hot.

Corny Corn Bread

Maybe this corn bread—a Richmond Street favorite—got its start when Coco the cook broiled too many ears of corn for his specialty, Enchiladas Rancheras (page 174). However it came to be, this recipe is a keeper. The corn kernels keep some of their pop even after baking in the corn bread.

MAKES: 8 TO 10 SERVINGS • PREP TIME: 15 MINUTES • COOK TIME: 30 MINUTES

3 ears corn on the cob

1½ cups fine yellow cornmeal

¾ cup all-purpose flour or white whole-wheat flour

2 tablespoons sugar

2 teaspoons baking powder

1 teaspoon kosher salt

½ teaspoon baking soda

¾ cup buttermilk

½ cup whole milk

2 large eggs

3 tablespoons melted butter

1 tablespoon butter, softened

1 tablespoon vegetable oil (if made in a cast-iron pan)

VARIATION FOR CHEESY-CORNY CORN BREAD:
Add ¾ cup shredded jack cheese to the batter along with the butter

1 Broil the corn and scrape the kernels from the cob according to the instructions for Enchiladas Rancheras on page 174. This may be done up to a day in advance and the kernels refrigerated.

2 Set the rack in the center position and preheat the oven to 400°F.

3 Stir the cornmeal, flour, sugar, baking powder, salt, and baking soda together in a mixing bowl. Toss in the broiled corn kernels until coated. If necessary, break any clusters of kernels apart with your fingers.

4 Beat the buttermilk, milk, and eggs together in a separate bowl until no streaks of yolks are visible. Pour the egg mixture into the dry ingredients and stir together with a rubber spatula, scraping down the bowl, just until blended. Stir in the melted butter. A few lumps are fine.

5 Heat 1 tablespoon butter and the vegetable oil in a 9-inch cast-iron skillet over low heat. (See note if baking in a cake pan instead of a skillet.) Turn up the heat under the pan until the butter is foaming. Scrape the batter into the pan. Handling it carefully, put the pan on the rack.

6 Whichever type of pan you use, bake until the top of the corn bread is light golden brown and the center springs back when pressed with a finger, about 25 minutes. Cool the corn bread on a rack at least 30 minutes before serving. Serve warm or at room temperature.

Note: The corn bread may be baked in a 9-inch cake pan. Simply grease the pan well with 1 tablespoon butter (omit the oil), flour lightly, and set aside until the batter is ready.

Orange Upside-Down Cake

Down in La Florida, the girls get their fill of oranges—in juice, cocktails, and this light and refreshing dessert. This is a fancy-looking cake, dense in texture but light in flavor, and it is so simple Blanche can pull it together while her nails are drying (as long as Rose does the measuring and Sofia does the dishes).

MAKES: ONE 9-INCH CAKE • PREP TIME: 20 MINUTES • COOK TIME: 30 MINUTES

FOR THE ORANGES AND SYRUP:
2 large oranges, seedless navel or Cara Cara

4 tablespoons (2 ounces) unsalted butter

½ packed cup light brown sugar

FOR THE CAKE:
2 cups all-purpose flour

1 teaspoon baking powder

½ teaspoon salt

¼ teaspoon baking soda

½ cup sour cream

½ cup whole milk

1 stick (4 ounces) unsalted butter, at room temperature

⅔ cup granulated sugar

2 eggs, at room temperature

½ teaspoon orange extract

1 Heat the oven to 350°F with a rack in the center position. Spray a 9-inch round cake pan with nonstick baking spray. Set aside.

PREP THE ORANGES AND SYRUP:
2 Cut the ends off the oranges. Stand one of the oranges on one of its flat ends on a cutting board. With a small sharp knife, cut away the peel and white pith, leaving as much of the rest of the orange intact as possible. Working over a small bowl, cut out the individual orange segments from between the membrane and let them drop into the bowl. After you've cut out all the segments, squeeze out the juice from the membrane into the bowl. Lift the segments onto a double thickness of paper towels to drain. Repeat with the other orange, and set the segments and juice aside separately.

3 Heat the butter and sugar in a heavy saucepan over low heat, stirring occasionally, until the syrup is bubbling. You'll notice the sugar isn't really dissolved and the butter isn't blended in. Add the orange juice to the simmering syrup and cook until the sugar is dissolved and the syrup is smooth and shiny, 4 to 5 minutes.

4 Pour about ⅔ of the syrup into the prepared cake pan and tilt the pan so the syrup covers the bottom evenly. Leave the rest of the syrup in the saucepan. Arrange some of the smaller orange segments in a very tight circle in the center of the pan and then a looser circle just outside the first circle. Put the cake pan in the refrigerator while making the batter.

MAKE THE CAKE:

5 Sift the flour, baking powder, salt, and baking soda together into a medium bowl. Measure the sour cream and milk into a liquid measuring cup and stir until blended.

6 With a handheld mixer, beat the butter, sugar, eggs, and orange extract together until smooth. Add half the sour cream mixture and mix just until blended in. Add half the flour mixture and blend just until no streaks of flour remain—don't overmix. Repeat with the remaining sour cream and flour mixtures, beating after each addition just until blended. Scrape the bottom and sides of the bowl with a rubber spatula and beat again just until the batter is smooth.

7 Spoon the batter into the pan gently—to keep the orange pattern intact—then very gently smooth out the batter.

8 Bake until the cake is risen and golden brown around the edges, about 35 minutes. Transfer the cake to a cooling rack and cool 30 to 45 minutes. Run a thin knife around the edge of the cake pan. Place the cooling rack over the cake and flip quickly to invert the cake onto the rack. Slowly lift the pan off the cake. It should come off easily. If any orange slices stick to the pan, just peel them off and put them back in place on the cake. Warm the remaining syrup in the pan over low heat and brush over the top of the fruit and cake. Cool completely before cutting and serving. The cake will last, wrapped in plastic and at room temperature, for at least 2 days.

GOLDEN WISDOM

As the cake bakes, it will push the orange segments toward the edges of the pan. So the segments don't "slip round the bend" onto the sides of the pan, keep them clustered in the center of the pan when you arrange them over the syrup.

Pecan Pie

Pecan pie is second only to cheesecake in the makes-everything-okay category. Wonderful an hour out of the oven (or rewarmed), at room temperature, or even out of the fridge. Serve with a scoop of vanilla ice cream or not, naked or with a dollop of whipped cream. Heck, there's no way not to enjoy pecan pie. This one has it all—sweetness but not too much, a gooey layer but, again, not too much, chopped pecans, whole pecans, a super-flaky but sturdy crust. All you need is friends—three of them, say—to enjoy it with.

MAKES: 8 TO 10 SERVINGS • PREP TIME: 15 MINUTES, PLUS TIME TO BAKE SHELL • BAKE TIME: 45 MINUTES ——

1 Prebaked Pie Shell (page 134) or 1 store-bought pie shell, baked according to directions in pie shell recipe

1 cup light brown sugar

3 eggs, at room temperature

1½ teaspoons vanilla extract

½ teaspoon salt

½ cup dark corn syrup

4 tablespoons unsalted butter, melted

1½ cups coarsely chopped pecans

½ cup pecan halves

1 Make, bake, and cool the pie shell. Heat the oven to 350°F.

2 Beat the brown sugar, eggs, vanilla, and salt together in a large bowl until very well blended and a little frothy. Beat in the corn syrup and butter until fully blended. Stir in the chopped pecans.

3 Pour the filling into the cooled crust. Decorate the top with the pecan halves however you like. Place the pie plate directly on the oven rack and bake until the center is jiggly but not liquid, about 45 minutes. (Test by gently wiggling the pie plate.) Remove to a cooling rack and cool completely before cutting. The pie can be stored covered and at room temperature for up to 2 days.

Prebaked Pie Shell

MAKES: 1 BOTTOM CRUST • PREP TIME: 25 MINUTES, PLUS CHILL TIME • BAKE TIME: 25 MINUTES

1½ cups all-purpose flour

1 tablespoon sugar

¼ teaspoon salt

4 tablespoons unsalted butter, cut into 4 pieces, chilled

3 tablespoons vegetable shortening, chilled

4 tablespoons ice water

1 Stir the flour, sugar, and salt together in a large bowl. Add the butter and shortening and toss. Using a pastry blender or your fingertips, work the butter and shortening into the flour. Continue until the mix looks like very coarse cornmeal with the occasional larger piece of fat. Refrigerate the mix for 15 minutes or so.

2 Sprinkle 3 tablespoons ice water over the flour mix while tossing with a fork until mixed well. Add ice water, a few drops at a time, while tossing until the dough holds together when pressed with your fingertips. Add just enough water to hold the dough together without making it soggy. When you think the dough is ready, pick up the whole batch and press gently together with your hands; the dough should hold together with just a few loose pieces falling back into the bowl. If it doesn't hold together, continue adding water, a few drops at a time, until it does.

3 Turn the dough out onto the countertop and, working quickly, knead the dough very gently to incorporate any loose bits. Press the dough into a circle and wrap it in plastic wrap. Refrigerate for at least 1 hour and up to 1 day.

 Wow, this crust recipe is so darn long, why not just go buy one?

4 When ready to bake the crust, heat the oven to 400°F with a rack in the lower position. Lightly butter a 9-inch pie dish.

5 On a lightly floured countertop, roll out the dough to a 12-inch circle. Flour the countertop and rolling pin as necessary to keep the dough from sticking. Gently fold the dough circle in quarters and center the point of the dough over the pie dish. Unfold the dough and adjust it so there is an equal amount of overhang on all sides. Lift the dough and press it gently into the corners of the pie plate. Trim the dough to an even ½- to ¾-inch of overhang all around the edge of the pie plate.

6 Fold the overhanging dough under the dough on the rim of the pie plate to make a double-thick, even lip. Crimp using your fingers or a fork. Chill for at least 30 minutes and up to 4 hours. If chilling for longer than 30 minutes, wrap the dough and pan in plastic wrap.

7 Cut a piece of parchment paper or aluminum foil to slightly larger than the pie plate. Press gently into the corners of the chilled pie shell. Fill the plate halfway with pie weights or uncooked beans or rice. Bake 15 minutes. Remove the paper or foil and weights. Poke the bottom of the pie shell with a fork about a dozen times around the edges and in the center. Return the pie shell to the oven and bake until pale golden brown, about 10 minutes. Cool completely before using.

Mint Julep Ice Cream

Dark brown sugar adds depth of flavor, like you get from bourbon aged in oak barrels. You will need an ice-cream maker to get the super-smooth texture that makes Blanche's Mint Julep the talk of Atlanta.

MAKES: 3½ CUPS OR ABOUT 4 SERVINGS • PREP TIME: 5 MINUTES • STEEP AND FREEZE TIME: 3 TO 4 HOURS

3 cups light cream

½ cup sugar

2 tablespoons dark brown sugar

¼ teaspoon salt

1 cup well-packed mint sprigs, stems and all, plus 4 beautiful sprigs for garnish

3 tablespoons bourbon

Confectioners' sugar

1 Bring the cream, sugar, brown sugar, and salt to a simmer, stirring occasionally to dissolve, over medium-low heat. Chop the mint sprigs very coarsely.

2 When the cream is simmering, remove from the heat. Squeeze the mint in your hands to bruise it and stir into the cream. Cover and let stand at least 2 and up to 4 hours. Strain the cream into a container, pressing on the leaves to extract as much goodness as possible. Chill completely.

3 Put a bowl with the bourbon in it in the freezer for at least 15 minutes. Freeze the ice cream according to the directions for your ice-cream freezer. Scoop into the bowl of bourbon and mix in the bourbon quickly. Transfer to a freezer storage container and freeze for at least 2 hours and up to 2 days.

4 To serve, lay out the reserved mint sprigs. Dust them very lightly with confectioners' sugar. Scoop the ice cream into pretty bowls, and garnish with the sugared mint sprigs.

GOLDEN WISDOM

If the bourbon were added to the ice-cream base, the ice cream would take much longer to freeze and ice crystals—the enemy of great ice cream—would have a chance to form. Here it is folded in at the end, and smooth ice cream with a kick wins the day.

Note: The amount of bourbon here will give you a pleasant background flavor that doesn't fight the mint. If you like a stronger mint julep, drizzle a little more bourbon over the top of each serving.

Blanche's Drink-It-Off Shake

When Blanche needed to fit into her (RED!) wedding dress for her and George's wedding anniversary, she turned to a diet that allowed her two shakes and a sensible meal per day. She stuck to her diet until Rose needed a snack and accidentally ate Blanche's tuna quiche meal, calling it "that little pie." Even worse, Rose had also consumed Blanche's last shake, explaining remorsefully, "I needed something to wash down the little pie. . . . It was so fishy!"

MAKES: ABOUT 2 CUPS OR 1 LARGE SERVING • PREP TIME: 5 MINUTES

1½ cups almond, soy, or oat milk

1 heaping cup frozen mango chunks

½ banana

1 tightly packed cup kale leaves

1½ teaspoons flax seeds

¼ cup oatmeal, optional

Put all ingredients in a blender in the order listed. Start blending on low speed. When the chunks of mango are no longer banging against the side of the blender, increase the speed to high and continue blending until the shake is perfectly smooth. Pour into a glass and enjoy.

Sloe Gin Fizz

Something smooth and sweet with a little kick to it, indeed. These are perfect for brunch or for a little something just around happy hour. If you can search out imported, specifically English, sloe gin, give it a try. It has more of the kick Dr. Elliot Clayton was looking for (and never got).

MAKES: 2 DRINKS • PREP TIME: 5 MINUTES

½ cup sloe gin

¼ cup lemon juice

6 to 8 ice cubes

Club soda or seltzer

Lime or lemon slice, optional

Pour the sloe gin and lemon juice into a cocktail shaker and add the ice. Shake very well and pour into 2 highball glasses, dividing the ice evenly. Pour in enough club soda or seltzer to fill the glasses. Pour from a little bit of a height for drama and more of a fizz. Add a lime or lemon slice if you like, and serve.

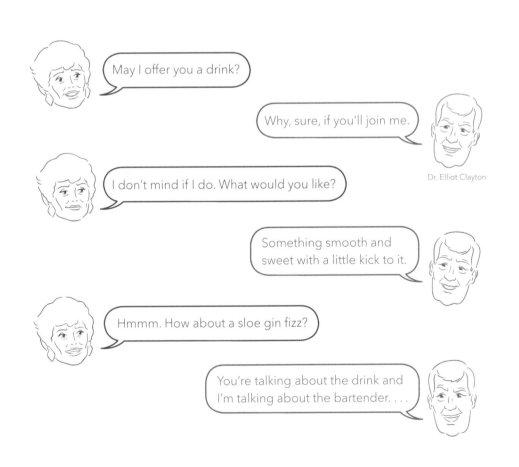

May I offer you a drink?

Why, sure, if you'll join me.

Dr. Elliot Clayton

I don't mind if I do. What would you like?

Something smooth and sweet with a little kick to it.

Hmmm. How about a sloe gin fizz?

You're talking about the drink and I'm talking about the bartender. . . .

Cherry Cheesecake Ice Cream

Get that ice-cream maker ready to churn! This sweet treat rolls two of the girls' favorites into one: rich, cheesecake-inspired ice cream studded with luscious cherries and bits of graham cracker crunchies.

MAKES: ABOUT 3½ CUPS • PREP TIME: 5 MINUTES • COOK TIME: 15 MINUTES • FREEZE TIME: 20 MINUTES ——

FOR THE ICE CREAM:

½ cup frozen dark cherries

6 ounces cream cheese

½ cup sour cream

1 teaspoon vanilla

2 cups whole milk

½ cup sugar

Large pinch salt

3 egg yolks

MAKE THE ICE-CREAM BASE:

1 Cut the cherries into quarters—they will be easy to cut even when frozen. Put them in a medium bowl and return them to the freezer. Cut the cream cheese into 8 pieces and put them in a heatproof bowl. Have the measured sour cream and vanilla nearby.

2 Heat the milk, sugar, and salt in a 2-quart saucepan over medium heat just until it begins to steam. Meanwhile, beat the yolks in a medium bowl until very well blended.

3 Pour about ¼ cup of the steaming milk into the yolks. Whisk well until blended. While whisking, pour another ½ cup or so of milk into the yolks. Pour the egg mixture into the saucepan and switch over to a heatproof rubber spatula. Stir, paying attention to the bottom, sides, and corners of the pan, until the custard thickens enough to coat a metal spoon lightly. This may take about 10 minutes, but don't be tempted to increase the heat. The idea is to heat the custard slowly. If you go too quickly, you will scramble the yolks. If you own an instant-read thermometer, which any Golden Girl should, you'll know the custard is almost there when it reaches 180°F.

4 Pour the finished custard over the cream cheese. Let sit 2 to 3 minutes, then whisk gently until the cream cheese is melted and blended into the custard. Gently whisk in the sour cream and vanilla. Pour the ice-cream base into a container (glass is better than plastic) with a piece of plastic wrap pressed directly onto the surface. Refrigerate until thoroughly chilled.

FOR THE GRAHAM STIR-INS:
4 whole (or 8 small) graham crackers

2 tablespoons sugar

1½ tablespoons melted butter

Large pinch fine salt

MAKE THE GRAHAM STIR-INS AND FINISH THE ICE CREAM:

5 Heat the oven to 350°F. Combine all stir-in ingredients in a food processor and process, stopping to scrape down the bowl a few times, until the graham crackers are very finely ground. Scrape the mix onto a baking sheet and pat into a 6-inch circle. Bake until lightly browned around the edges, about 12 minutes. Remove and cool, then put the whole tray in the freezer. Freeze until solid.

6 Pour the chilled custard into your ice-cream freezer and freeze according to the manufacturer's instructions. While the ice cream is freezing, use a fork to break the stir-ins into small pieces (about the size of large peas). Keep in the freezer.

7 Scoop the ice cream into the bowl of cherries, sprinkle the stir-ins over the top, and fold both into the ice cream just enough to make sure they are evenly mixed. Scrape the ice cream into a container and freeze for at least 2 hours.

8 To serve, test the ice cream to see if it is scoopable. If not, let stand at room temperature for about 5 minutes or in the refrigerator for about 10 minutes.

Nils Feelander attempted to harass me repeatedly.

What do you mean, he attempted to?

He worked at Lars Erikson's Drugstore and Tackle Shop. He was the soda jerk. Now that I think about it, he was the town jerk! Every Saturday afternoon I'd go in and have a sundae. Well, Nils would arrange the ice-cream scoops in an obscene way. I could never prove it, because by the time I would take it home to show my father, the evidence had—

Melted.

Melted.

Yeah. To this day, every time I pass an ice-cream parlor or a tackle shop, I blush!

Sophia

But you have to promise me you won't do anything to embarrass me.

I'll try, but if they serve me cauliflower, it's in God's hands.

Whether it's a lasagna for her gentleman friend at the center, zabaglione for her brother Angelo, or a rum cake just for the hell of it, Sophia is very comfortable in the kitchen. From morning until evening (or from String Beans and Scrambled Eggs to Speedy Spiedini) Sophia has a dish to offer everyone, any time of day.

All these recipes are a mix of her Sicilian heritage—she grew up around people who cooked as much as she does—and her need to provide for a growing family when she and Sal were starting out in Brooklyn. There are filling and inexpensive dishes like Escarole and White Beans, Chunky Minestrone, and Mussels Fra Diavolo over spaghetti.

There are also special-occasion dishes like Lasagna al Forno, Gorgonzola Mushrooms, and a huge platter of Antipasto Salad. And for Sunday dinner, there's Sunday Gravy, with its meaty mix of sausages, braciole, and meatballs simmered in an authentic, slow-cooked tomato sauce.

But not all of Sophia's best recipes come from the island of Sicily. At least one comes from the island of Coney, like Max Weinstock's knishes. And Sophia, though not a huge fan of Mexican food, loved Coco's Enchiladas Rancheras so much, she asked for the recipe.

Leave some room for dessert, like the delightful Carrot Cake Goes to Miami—an orange-juice-and-mango version of the classic. You didn't save that much room? Nibble on a Citrus-Almond Biscotti and sip on an Amaretto Sour.

Whether you're cooking for an army, like Sophia usually does, or simply putting delicious food on the table for just a few friends and loved ones, there is something for you in Sophia's recipe box.

String Beans and Scrambled Eggs

It might sound like a crazy combination, but Sophia made this simple, delicious breakfast treat whenever her grandkids had a sleepover. Cooking the eggs slowly in olive oil gives them a creamy texture that kids love, and the string beans add a savory deliciousness.

MAKES: 2 SERVINGS • PREP TIME: 5 MINUTES • COOK TIME: 10 MINUTES

2 tablespoons olive oil

1 cup cooked string beans, cut into 1-inch lengths

½ cup thinly sliced yellow onion

4 eggs

Fine sea or kosher salt and freshly ground black pepper

1   Heat the olive oil over medium-low heat in a medium nonstick pan. Add the string beans and onions, season lightly with salt and pepper, and cook, stirring occasionally, until the onion is softened and the beans are sizzling gently, about 4 minutes.

2   Meanwhile, beat the eggs in a medium bowl with a pinch each of salt and pepper.

3   Pour the eggs into the pan and cook, stirring with a heatproof spatula, until the eggs are firm but still creamy, about 5 minutes. Taste and add a little salt and pepper if needed. Serve hot, with toast.

I will not have that filthy beast in my house! It belongs in a barnyard.

This is not a farm chicken. Count Bessie is a showbiz chicken.

Vegetable and Provolone Strata

Sophia is not a morning person. She doesn't appear to be an evening person, either. Here's a way for her to at least appear a little cheerful at breakfast with the girls: split the preparation time of the morning's meal. Here's how: Put the strata together in the evening so it can soak overnight, then top it and pop it in the oven in the AM. There's another advantage to this method—the strata takes on a lovely, almost custardy texture with all that soaking. See note on page 149 for shorter soaking options.

MAKES: 4 TO 6 SERVINGS • PREP TIME: 35 MINUTES, PLUS SOAK TIME • COOK TIME: 45 TO 50 MINUTES (UNATTENDED)

Butter, optional, for greasing the pan

2 tablespoons plus 2 teaspoons olive oil, plus more for greasing the pan, if using

1 large red or yellow bell pepper, cored, seeded, and diced into ½-inch pieces (about 2 cups)

1 large yellow or red onion, diced into 1-inch pieces (about 1¼ cups)

1 teaspoon fine sea or kosher salt, plus more for seasoning the vegetables

One 10-ounce container cremini mushrooms, trimmed and cut in half, if large, then into ½-inch slices (about 3 cups)

¼ teaspoon freshly ground black pepper, plus more for seasoning the vegetables

1 cup cherry or grape tomatoes, halved

5 cups 1-inch bread cubes, preferably dense, whole-wheat bread

3 cups milk

1 Heat the oven to 400°F. Lightly butter or grease with olive oil an 11 x 8-inch baking dish.

2 Heat 2 tablespoons olive oil in a large sauté pan over medium-low heat. Add the pepper and onion, season lightly with salt, and cook until softened, about 8 minutes. Add the mushrooms and cook, stirring until the onions and peppers are tender, about 10 minutes. If the mushrooms give off a lot of liquid, increase the heat slightly and continue cooking. There should be no liquid left in the pan by the time the vegetables are tender. Season the vegetables with salt and pepper and set them aside to cool.

3 Put the cherry tomatoes on a small baking sheet and drizzle 2 teaspoons olive oil over them. Season generously with salt and pepper, and toss to coat with the oil and seasoning. Turn them cut side up and roast until lightly browned and sizzling, about 15 minutes. Remove and cool.

4 Spread the bread cubes out on a baking sheet. Bake just to toast them up a little, about 12 minutes. (This can be done while the tomatoes are roasting.)

5 Whisk the milk, eggs, 1 teaspoon salt, and ¼ teaspoon pepper together in a large bowl. Add the vegetable mix, bread cubes, shredded provolone, and baby arugula. Mix well and turn into the prepared baking dish. Cover and refrigerate for at least 1 hour and up to overnight (see note).

8 eggs

2 cups shredded sharp or mild provolone

One 5-ounce container baby arugula

¼ cup shredded Parmesan

6 When ready to bake, heat the oven to 350°F with a rack in the center position.

7 Arrange the tomatoes, cut side up, on the top of the strata. Sprinkle the Parmesan over all. Bake until the center is firm, about 50 minutes. Cool at least 15 minutes before serving.

Note: Shorter soaking times will yield a strata with firmer bread cubes and a more custardy egg and vegetable mix. The longer soaking time makes a more homogenous strata with almost no unabsorbed egg and a firm texture. In-between soaking times will yield a strata with in-between texture. All are delicious; it's just a question of taste.

PASTA ONE-TWO-THREE

Here are three simple steps that will make any pasta dish you cook better. Guaranteed.

FIRST
Never dump pasta onto a platter or plate and then spoon the sauce over it. Pasta and sauce need a little time together in the pan so they can get acquainted. If you're starting out with cold sauce, warm it up gently while the pasta is cooking. After draining the pasta, return it to the pan and add the sauce. Whatever the sauce, there should be just enough of it to lightly coat the pasta (if not, see below), so hold some back if you see the pasta might become over-sauced. You can always pass the extra at the table.

SECOND
Remove about 1 cup of the pasta cooking water before draining the pasta. You probably won't use this much, but better too much than not enough. Spoon a little of the reserved water into the pan with the pasta and sauce and bring it to a good boil. Toss the pasta around—if it doesn't glide in the sauce, add a little more of the water. This addition of water finishes the cooking of the pasta in the sauce and gives the pasta a chance to start absorbing the sauce.

THIRD
Finish off the pasta with a little butter or olive oil and a little grated cheese, if you like. Before you do either, remove the pan from the heat. Add the butter/oil and cheese and stir to mix them in. That's it. Take these three steps with your favorite pasta sauce, whether homemade or store-bought.

Chunky Minestrone

MAKES: 12 CUPS OR 8 SERVINGS • PREP TIME: 45 MINUTES • COOK TIME: 45 TO 55 MINUTES

⅓ cup olive oil

2 medium yellow onions, cut into 1-inch chunks (about 3 cups)

3 medium carrots, peeled and cut into ½-inch rounds (about 1½ cups)

2 stalks celery, trimmed and cut into 1-inch chunks (about 1½ cups)

One 10-ounce package medium white or cremini mushrooms, trimmed and quartered (about 3 cups)

Fine sea salt

Half a small head (about 1½ pounds) savoy cabbage, core removed, leaves shredded ½-inch thick (about 6 cups)

2 large parsnips or medium white turnips, peeled and cut into ¾-inch chunks (about 2 cups)

8 cups store-bought chicken broth or Rotisserie Chicken Broth (page 71)

2 small zucchini, trimmed and cut into ¾-inch chunks (about 2 cups)

½ pound string beans, ends trimmed, cut into 1-inch lengths (about 2 cups)

One 15-ounce can diced tomatoes

One 15-ounce can cannellini beans or chickpeas, drained and rinsed

1 cup frozen peas

1 cup small pasta shapes, like acini di pepe, tubetti, or orzo

Freshly ground black pepper

1 Heat the olive oil in a 5- to 6-quart heavy pot or Dutch oven over medium heat. Add the onions, carrots, celery, and mushrooms, and season them lightly with salt. Cook, stirring often, until they are done steaming and begin to sizzle, about 8 minutes. Stir in the cabbage and parsnips or turnips and cook, stirring often, until the cabbage is wilted, about 5 minutes.

2 Add the chicken broth, zucchini, string beans, tomatoes, canned beans, and peas. Increase the heat to high and bring to a boil. Season to taste with salt. Adjust the heat so the liquid is at a gentle boil, cover the pot, and cook until all the vegetables are tender, about 10 minutes. The soup may be prepared to this point up to three days in advance. Cool it to room temperature, then refrigerate it right in the pot. Bring to a simmer over low heat before continuing.

3 Bring a medium saucepan of salted water to a boil. Stir in the pasta and cook, stirring occasionally, until al dente, 6 to 10 minutes, depending on the pasta shape you choose. Drain the pasta and stir it into the soup. Stir gently until the pasta is heated through, a minute or two.

4 Taste the soup and add salt and pepper if you like. Ladle the hot soup into warm bowls and serve immediately. Pass any extras you choose separately at the table, allowing the rest of the girls to help themselves.

GOLDEN WISDOM

Cooking the pasta separately prevents it from swelling up and overtaking your soup. If you plan to refrigerate or freeze all or part of the soup, do so before adding the pasta.

Every Golden Girl knows it's the little extras that help make a meal. Serve the minestrone with any or all of these: Basil-Arugula Pesto (recipe follows), grated Parmesan, extra-virgin olive oil, Bruschetta, or Salad Croutons (page 159).

Basil-Arugula Pesto

Adding arugula to a traditional pesto gives it a little peppery nip, which goes nicely with most soups, especially minestrone. Try some on sandwiches and a little spooned into salad dressings.

MAKES: ABOUT 1 CUP • PREP TIME: 15 MINUTES

3 cups lightly packed basil leaves

1 cup lightly packed arugula leaves (large is better for this than baby, but baby will do)

1 clove garlic, peeled and smashed

½ cup walnut pieces

½ teaspoon fine sea salt

½ cup good olive oil, plus more for floating on top of the finished pesto

½ cup grated good-quality Parmesan cheese (measured after grating with a rasp-style grater)

1 Wash the basil and arugula in plenty of cool water. Both can be quite sandy/gritty. Spin them dry and then lay them out in a single layer on paper towels. Loosely roll up the basil and arugula and store them in the refrigerator for up to a day.

2 Put the basil, arugula, and garlic in a high-speed blender or food processor. Process until the greens are finely chopped. Add the walnuts and salt and, with the motor running, drizzle in the oil in a steady stream. Add the grated Parmesan and pulse a few times to mix the cheese into the pesto.

3 Scrape the pesto into a small glass bowl. Check for taste and add a little salt if needed. Float a thin layer of olive oil on top of the pesto and cover with plastic wrap, pressing the wrap directly to the surface of the oil. The pesto may be refrigerated for up to 4 days or frozen in small portions up to 2 months.

In Sicily, we never went to the doctor. We went to the Widow Caravelli. Whatever you had, she had a cure. She was most famous for her green salve to cure ear infections. One day, she gave some to Salvadore, an idiot. He misunderstood the directions and put it on his linguine instead of in his ear.

Well, I guess if you're an idiot with a hearing problem, you do things like that.

Actually, it turned out okay. The stuff tasted great, so Salvadore decided to market it. At first, things didn't go so well. Linguine with ear salve wasn't very appetizing—but once he changed the name to pesto sauce, it sold like hotcakes!

Antipasto Salad

What are two great ways to start an Italian meal? Crunchy greens with a tart red wine vinegar dressing and a bountiful antipasto platter. You don't have to decide between the two, either—serve both!

MAKES: 6 SERVINGS • PREP TIME: 30 MINUTES

FOR THE DRESSING:

½ cup olive oil (this is the time to break out the good stuff)

2 tablespoons red wine vinegar

¾ teaspoon fine sea or kosher salt

½ teaspoon dried oregano, optional

¼ teaspoon freshly ground black pepper

FOR THE SALAD:

8 cups greens, cut into bite-size pieces, washed and spun dry

8 to 10 whole pepperoncinis, drained

8 to 10 medium pitted green olives

16 cherry tomatoes, halved

12 medium-thick slices sweet sopressata or pepperoni, cut into ½-inch strips

½ head fennel, trimmed well and cut into thin slices

1 piece aged, sharp provolone, for shaving

MAKE THE DRESSING:

Put the olive oil, vinegar, salt, oregano (if using), and pepper into a small jar with a tight-fitting lid. Shake well. The dressing may be made up to 4 hours in advance and kept at room temperature, or up to a day in advance and refrigerated. If refrigerated, bring the dressing to room temperature an hour before serving.

MAKE THE SALAD:

Make an even layer of the greens in a wide, shallow serving bowl. Arrange the pepperoncinis, olives, cherry tomatoes, sopressata, and fennel in a spoke pattern over the greens, or simply scatter them over the greens. Using a vegetable peeler, shave as much or little of the provolone over the salad as you like. Bring the salad to the table. Give the dressing a good shake and drizzle most of it over the salad. Toss well, taste a piece of the greens, and add more dressing if you like. Toss again and serve.

GOLDEN WISDOM

Choose some bold greens like radicchio, arugula, and endive to stand up to the flavors of the other salad ingredients, and a measure of romaine for crunch.

Max Weinstock's Secret Potato Knish Recipe

It was a tragedy: Max Weinstock and Sal Petrillo's pizza and knish stand going out of business because of Sal's gambling problem. The situation sparked a bitter feud between Max and Sophia. Max never told her the truth, and placed the blame on himself to keep Sal and Sophia's marriage together. When Max finally came clean, Sophia forgave him (sort of). And then Max did the unthinkable—he handed over the recipes for the best knishes in Brooklyn.

MAKES: 4 TO 6 KNISHES • PREP TIME: 45 MINUTES, PLUS REST TIME • COOK TIME: 30 MINUTES

FOR THE DOUGH:

1¾ cups all-purpose flour, plus more for kneading

1 teaspoon kosher salt

½ cup lukewarm water, or as needed

¼ cup vegetable oil

FOR THE POTATO-ONION FILLING:

2 large russet potatoes (about 1¼ pounds), peeled and cut into ½-inch slices

Kosher salt

2 tablespoons vegetable oil

2 garlic cloves, chopped very fine

2 medium yellow onions, cut into ¼-inch strips (about 4 cups)

Freshly ground black pepper

3 tablespoons melted butter

Vegetable oil

Sour cream, if you like

Sliced scallions, green and white parts, if you like

MAKE THE DOUGH:

1 Stir the flour and salt together in a bowl. Make a well in the center and pour in ⅓ cup of the water and ¼ cup oil. Beat the water and oil together with a fork and then gradually beat the flour into the liquid. Continue mixing in flour until the mixture gets too thick to beat with a fork, then mix it with your hands into a rough dough. Knead in some or all of the remaining water if you find the mixture isn't coming together into a smooth dough.

2 Turn the dough out onto a lightly floured countertop and knead, adding flour as necessary, until the dough is very smooth and no longer spotty (meaning the oil and water are blended into the dough evenly). This could take up to 10 minutes. Cut the dough in half. Wrap the halves in plastic wrap. Leave one at room temperature while making the filling, and freeze the other (see note).

MAKE THE FILLING:

3 Put the potatoes in a saucepan of cold water. Add a heaping teaspoon of salt, and bring the water to a boil over high heat. Adjust the heat so the water is simmering, and cook until the potatoes are barely tender, about 10 minutes. Drain the potatoes and keep at room temperature.

4 Heat 2 tablespoons vegetable oil in a large skillet over medium heat. Add the garlic and fry to a pale golden color (this will take only a minute or so). Add the onions, season lightly with salt, and stir until they are softened, about 5 minutes. Adjust the heat to medium-low and continue cooking until the onions are just beginning to brown, about 15 minutes.

5 Add the drained potatoes and stir to break them up into small chunks. (Don't overmix; you want a little texture, yes, bubala?) Season with salt and pepper, and cool before using.

FORM AND COOK THE KNISHES:

6 On a lightly floured countertop, roll the refrigerated half of the dough out to a 16 x 10-inch rectangle. You should be able to see through the dough in spots when finished rolling. Pull gently to thin out thicker spots and to make a fairly even rectangle. Let the dough rest 10 minutes.

7 Brush the top of the dough with about half of the melted butter. Position the dough so one of the long sides is closest to you. Make a line of the filling about 1½ inches from the edge closest to you that runs to within 1 inch of the shorter ends. Pat the filling into an even mound. Fold the edge of the dough closest to you over the filling and, using your hands with spread-out fingers, roll the dough and filling into a fairly tight roll. Pinch the loose edge of the dough that runs the length of the roll to seal. Cut the ends of the roll to about ½ inch from the filling.

8 Using the side of your hand, gently karate chop the roll to make indentations that mark it into 6 even portions (4 portions for a larger knish). Wiggle the side of your hand to nudge the filling to either side of the indentations. Cut the roll into portions using the center of the indentations for a guide. Working with one knish at a time, pinch the dough together on one cut side. Stand the knish up on its pinched end and press it gently to flatten the bottom. Separate the dough on the top of the knish to expose some of the filling. Shape the knish sides into a more or less round shape. Set the finished knish on a plate lined with plastic wrap. Repeat with the rest of the knishes. The knishes may be made up to several hours in advance, covered with plastic wrap, and refrigerated. They may also be frozen for up to 2 months. If freezing, refrigerate the formed knishes first until firm. Wrap the knishes first in plastic wrap and then in foil before freezing.

9 Heat the oven to 400°F with a rack in the center position.

10 Brush the tops and sides of the knishes with the remaining butter. Pour enough vegetable oil into a large ovenproof skillet (cast iron is ideal!) to make an even ⅛-inch or so layer in the bottom. Heat over medium heat until rippling. Carefully slip as many of the knishes as will fit into the skillet, top side down, without touching. Cook, without moving, until you can see the edges of the tops beginning to brown. Turn the knishes and cook for 2 minutes. Put the skillet in the oven and cook until the undersides are golden brown and the sides are crisp, about 25 minutes. Remove the skillet carefully. Transfer the knishes to a serving plate and let cool for 10 minutes before serving. Top with a dollop of sour cream and scallions if you like.

Note: This dough freezes beautifully. Defrost in the refrigerator overnight before using. Either make this same filling again or wait for a windfall of leftover mashed potatoes and stir in some sautéed onions or anything else you'd like.

———————————— GOLDEN WISDOM ————————————

As you roll, add flour, a little at a time, when needed to keep the dough from sticking. You'll need very little flour; the oil in the dough will keep it from sticking to the countertop.

Mussels Fra Diavolo

On their own or with a little crusty bread, spicy mussels in broth make a nice appetizer. Over spaghetti, they make a meal.

MAKES: 2 TO 4 SERVINGS • PREP TIME: 10 MINUTES • COOK TIME: 6 TO 8 MINUTES

2 tablespoons olive oil

2 cloves garlic, sliced

¼ to ½ teaspoon crushed red pepper (optional)

One 8-ounce can tomato sauce

1½ pounds cultivated mussels

¼ cup chopped Italian parsley leaves

Kosher or sea salt to taste

Crusty bread or Bruschetta (page 159), for serving

1 Heat the olive oil in a heavy 3-quart saucepan or Dutch oven over medium heat. (For the pan, wider and shallower is better.) Add the garlic and ¼ teaspoon red pepper. Fry until the garlic is fragrant, about 1 minute.

2 Add the tomato sauce and ½ cup water. Heat to boiling, then reduce the heat to simmering. Simmer, covered, 5 minutes.

3 Meanwhile, scrub the mussel shells with a stiff brush, getting into the crevices to remove all grit. Pull out the beards, if any, from halfway along the flat sides of the shells.

4 Increase the heat to high. When the zuppa is boiling, stir in the parsley. Add the cleaned mussels and cover tightly. Steam, shaking the pan occasionally, just until the shells open, 3 to 4 minutes. Taste the sauce and add salt and more red pepper if you think the sauce needs it. Spoon the rest of the sauce over the mussels and serve hot with crusty bread.

GOLDEN WISDOM

Those little-bitty 8-ounce cans of tomato sauce you see in the canned tomato aisle are ideal pantry-stockers. Stick with the plain tomato sauce and you can use them for all kinds of dishes where you want just a little bit of pure tomato flavor. These 15-minute mussels are one good example. The sauce will pick up flavor from the garlic and parsley, briny sweetness from the mussels, and zip from the red pepper.

Note: Prepare through step two up to 2 days in advance. Reheat the tomato base in a 3-quart saucepan. Check the seasonings and continue with the recipe.

VARIATION: CLAMS FRA DIAVOLO

Substitute 24 littleneck clams for the mussels. Scrub the shells under cold water, getting into the crevices. Add 2 to 3 minutes to the cooking time and expect that it will take 2 to 3 minutes for all the clams to open.

VARIATION: CLAMS OR MUSSELS FRA DIAVOLO OVER SPAGHETTI
Serves 3 to 4

Heat a large pot of salted water to boiling over high heat. Prepare the clams or mussels as directed above. When the shellfish goes in the pan, stir 8 ounces (half a 1-pound package) of spaghetti or linguine into the water. Cook to al dente—usually 1 to 2 minutes less than package directions—and drain. Return the pasta to the pot, mix in a little of the sauce, and turn the pasta out onto a platter. Top with the shellfish and sauce. See Pasta One-Two-Three on page 149 for more pointers on marrying pasta and sauce.

SOPHIA'S GUIDE TO CROUTONS, BRUSCHETTA, AND CROSTINI ———

If your old address is "Two miles west of Palermo, underneath the old bridge," you can bet you know the meaning of frugal. Here are a few of the ways Sophia turns bread into meal-changing toasts.

SALAD CROUTONS

Cut a stale loaf of French or Italian bread into ½-inch cubes. (Slice the crust off first or leave it on, as you like.) Drizzle olive oil—not too much—around the inside of a medium bowl. Add the bread cubes to the bowl and toss to coat them very lightly with the oil. Add herbs and finely grated cheese if you like. Season lightly with salt and pepper. Spread out the cubes on a baking sheet and bake in a 375°F oven, turning and stirring once, until golden brown, about 15 minutes. Cool. Croutons can be stored in an airtight container for up to 3 days.

BRUSCHETTA

Before you grab your bus pass to go meet Sophia at the center, know your stuff: Bruschetta are toasts, lightly charred in spots, that can be topped with any number of concoctions or floated on soups or stews—not the tomato topping that often goes on them. To make bruschetta, cut a loaf of dense-textured country bread on the diagonal into ¾ slices. Brush them lightly with olive oil and grill until golden brown and crispy with charred edges. (Bruciare means "to burn" in Italian.) Alternatively, you may toast the bread in a heavy skillet—cast iron is ideal—over medium heat until the centers are golden and the edges are lightly charred. Use within a few hours of making.

CROSTINI

Related to bruschetta, crostini are a little thinner and toasted until golden brown and crisp throughout. (Bruschetta are sometimes still soft in the center.) Cut long, thin loaves of dense country or whole-wheat bread into ½-inch slices. Lightly brush on both sides with olive oil. Arrange in a single layer on a baking sheet. Bake on the lowest rack of a 400°F oven until the underside is golden brown, about 12 minutes. Remove and cool. If you like, rub the brown side of the bread very lightly with a garlic clove.

Spaghetti Carbonara

Sophia knows that carbonara waits for no man. Especially if that man is Stanley, knocking on the door to announce a new get-rich-quick scheme. Once the eggs go in, it's time to eat!

MAKES: 4 SERVINGS • PREP TIME: 10 MINUTES • COOK TIME: 10 MINUTES

6 not-too-thin slices pancetta (about 3 ounces)

2 tablespoons olive oil

1 medium yellow onion, diced into ½-inch pieces (about 1½ cups)

¾ pound spaghetti

6 to 8 tablespoons finely grated pecorino Romano cheese (see note)

2 eggs, lightly beaten

Coarsely ground black pepper

1 Bring a large pot of lightly salted water to a boil. Meanwhile, unroll the pancetta slices and cut them crosswise into ½-inch strips. Cut the strips crosswise into ½-inch pieces.

2 Heat the olive oil in a large, deep skillet over medium-low heat. Add the onion and cook, stirring, until the onion is translucent but not browned, about 6 minutes. Add the pancetta and cook, stirring, until browned very lightly around the edges, about 4 minutes. (The onion should color only very lightly. If the onion begins to brown, lower the heat.) Remove the skillet from the heat.

3 Stir the spaghetti into the boiling water. Cook, stirring occasionally, until al dente—tender but with a little bite, about 7 minutes. Ladle off about ½ cup water and set it aside. Drain the pasta.

4 Return the skillet to the heat. When the onion and pancetta are sizzling, add the spaghetti and toss to coat with the pan juices. If there isn't enough to coat the spaghetti easily, add a little of the reserved water and toss again. Remove the pan from the heat, add the Romano and beaten eggs, and toss until the pasta is coated and the egg is no longer raw. If necessary, add a little more of the pasta cooking water to make enough sauce to lightly coat the pasta without looking thick. Season generously with black pepper and serve immediately, right from the pot into warm bowls.

Note: Change the amount or type of cheese to suit your preferences. If you don't like the sharp tang of Romano cheese, use Parmesan instead. Whatever cheese you decide on, taste it before you add it. If it seems very salty, start with less and pass the rest separately.

Speedy Spiedini

MAKES: 4 SERVINGS • PREP TIME: 10 MINUTES, PLUS 4+ HOURS MARINATING TIME • COOK TIME: 15 MINUTES

½ pound small cremini mushrooms

3 tablespoons olive oil

2 tablespoons coarsely chopped fresh rosemary or 1 tablespoon chopped fresh thyme

1½ teaspoons coarse salt (Maldon or kosher work well)

¼ teaspoon (a little more if you know your crowd) crushed red pepper flakes

12 multicolor grape tomatoes (pick the largest ones from the container) or large cherry tomatoes

1½ pounds boneless skinless chicken breast, cut into 1-inch cubes

Optional but nice: Big, colorful salad dressed with 1-2-3 Citrus Dressing (page 119), dressing from Caesar a la Zbornak (page 13), or Basil-Arugula Pesto (page 152)

——GOLDEN WISDOM——

Marinating the vegetables and chicken before they go on the skewers makes it easier to toss and coat more of the surface area. More coating = more flavor.

1 Wipe the cremini mushroom caps with a damp paper towel. Cut them in roughly about 1½-inch pieces. If they are cut too small, they will not stay on the skewers.

2 Whisk the olive oil, rosemary or thyme, salt, and pepper flakes together in a small bowl. Pour about half the marinade into a storage container that will fit the vegetables. Add the tomatoes and the cut-up mushrooms. Toss gently until coated. Repeat in a separate container with the remaining half of the marinade and the chicken. Cover the containers and refrigerate at least 4 hours and up to 1 day.

3 Bring the chicken and vegetables to room temperature about 30 minutes before cooking. Heat the oven to 425°F. Thread the chicken and vegetables onto 12 short (about 6-inch) skewers, varying the arrangements. (If you're using wooden skewers, soak them in cool water while the spiedini ingredients are marinating.) Oil a grill pan lightly and heat the pan over medium-low heat while assembling the spiedini.

4 Add as many spiedini as will fit in the pan/griddle without touching. Cook until the underside has nice grill marks, about 4 minutes. Flip and repeat. Place on a baking sheet. Do a second round of spiedini if necessary and add them to the baking sheet.

5 Bake the spiedini until the chicken is cooked through (an instant-read thermometer inserted into the center of a piece of chicken reads 165°F or higher). Serve warm.

Note: The spiedini may be cooked on an outdoor grill. With a gas grill on high or over very hot coals, mark the spiedini on two sides as described above. Lower the heat or move the spiedini to a cooler part of the grill and cover the grill. Finish cooking as described above.

Linguine with White Clam Sauce

Over the years, Sophia has come up with a clam sauce that has a little something for everyone. Some clams in the shell, some out, and even a dab of butter for extra richness.

MAKES: 2 TO 4 SERVINGS • PREP TIME: 15 MINUTES • COOK TIME: 15 MINUTES

36 littleneck clams (about 4 pounds; the littler the necks, the better)

½ cup dry white wine

¼ cup olive oil

1 medium clove garlic, sliced thin

¼ teaspoon crushed red pepper flakes

8 ounces (half package) linguine

1 tablespoon butter, at room temperature

¼ cup thinly sliced scallion greens or coarsely chopped Italian parsley leaves

Freshly ground black pepper

Kosher salt, if necessary

1 Scrub the clams under cold running water, making sure to get into the crevices. Drain.

2 Pour the wine into a large heavy pot and gently add the clams. Cover the pot tightly and bring the wine to a boil over high heat. Steam until the clams start to open, 7 to 8 minutes. Lift the lid and transfer the open clams to a bowl. Cover the pot and repeat until all the clams are open. If any clams remain closed after you've given them a poke, toss them.

3 Set aside the 12 smallest clams in their shells. Pull the remaining clams from the shells and discard the shells. Leave the clams whole or chop them very coarsely–your call. Strain the cooking liquid through cheesecloth or a coffee filter. Pour ½ cup over the shucked clams. Freeze the rest for clam chowder or a very delicious addition to a Bloody Mary. Prepare the clams in advance and leave them at room temperature up to 3 hours.

4 Heat a large pot of generously salted water to boiling over high heat. Set a colander in the sink.

5 Heat the olive oil in a large, deep sauté pan over medium-low heat. Add the garlic. When it begins to sizzle gently, add the pepper flakes. Lower the heat and pull the pan from the heat for a minute if the garlic is sizzling too vigorously. Cook until the sizzling stops, without browning the garlic. Add the shucked clams and their liquid. Simmer 4 minutes while cooking the pasta.

6 Add the linguine to the boiling water. Stir with a large fork or pair of tongs until all strands are submerged and separated. Boil until the linguine is tender but still firm in the center, about 7 minutes.

7 Remove ½ cup or so of the cooking water. Drain the pasta in a colander, shaking to remove excess water. Return the pasta to the pot, place over low heat, and add the clam sauce, butter, and clams in the shell. Stir until the pasta is coated with sauce. If necessary, add enough of the pasta cooking water to make enough creamy sauce to lightly coat the pasta. Check for seasoning and add salt, if needed, and black pepper to taste.

8 Transfer to a warmed platter and top with scallions or parsley. Serve immediately (with tongs is easiest).

Rich Meat Sauce

MAKES: ABOUT 7 CUPS • PREP TIME: 15 MINUTES • COOK TIME: 2½ TO 3½ HOURS (MOSTLY UNATTENDED) ——

Two 28-ounce cans of whole California or imported Italian plum tomatoes (about 5½ cups; see notes)

3 tablespoons olive oil

1 medium yellow onion, chopped (about 1 cup)

3 medium to large garlic cloves, sliced thin

½ pound ground beef plus ½ pound ground pork OR 1 pound either ground beef or ground pork

2 bay leaves

Fine sea or kosher salt and ground black pepper

Crushed red pepper flakes, optional

——— GOLDEN WISDOM ———

If you want to be finicky like Sophia, locate the core on each tomato and pinch it between your thumb and forefinger to remove it. If you pull the core out slowly, most likely many of the seeds will follow along, killing two birds with one stone.

1 Pour the tomatoes and juice into a large bowl. Squish the tomatoes one by one in your hand until they are roughly crushed. Return them to the juice. Keep fishing around until you're sure all the tomatoes are crushed.

2 Heat the olive oil in a deep, heavy 5-quart pan (not too tall and not too wide) over medium-low heat. Add the onion and garlic and stir until softened—not browned—about 6 minutes. Add ground meat and cook, breaking it up, until cooked through and the liquid is evaporated—the meat will stop steaming and begin to sizzle gently. Don't brown.

3 Pour the tomatoes and juice into the pan and add the bay leaves. Season lightly with salt and pepper. Heat to boiling, then adjust the heat so the sauce is barely simmering. Cook 2½ to 3½ hours, stirring occasionally, paying special attention to the corners of the pan. If the sauce sticks or thickens too much for your liking, add about ½ cup water to the pan. You may have several additions of water or just one or two. At the end of cooking, the tomatoes should have broken down quite a bit and the sauce should be thick, but not thick enough to stand a spoon in.

4 Taste the sauce and add salt and pepper and a dash of crushed red pepper if you like. The sauce will taste better if you let it sit off the heat for a couple of hours before reheating and serving. Or the sauce may be refrigerated up to 5 days or frozen for up to 3 months.

Notes: What kind of tomatoes to use for pasta sauce is an extremely personal choice. You would think Sophia favors Italian tomatoes, but California tomatoes were on sale at the supermarket and Sophia thought, *Oh, what the hell. Let's give it a shot.* American-grown tomatoes have a good balance of acidity and sweetness and a firm texture that can withstand long cooking.

This recipe makes enough to sauce 2 pounds of pasta (easily) or put together Lasagna al Forno (recipe follows) with spare sauce to pass at the table.

Lasagna al Forno

Picture it! Brooklyn, 1950. Sophia in a tiny Brooklyn kitchen, a pot of water coming to a boil, colander in place in the sink, and a bowl of cold water on the kitchen table (the one with the cigar box of silverware in the drawer). It must be lasagna day! Now Sophia does what so many other cooks do: make a lasagna with uncooked noodles and a slightly thinner sauce. The extra liquid in the sauce cooks the lasagna while it's baking. POOF! Lasagna in less than half the time!

MAKES: 12 SERVINGS • PREP TIME: 15 MINUTES • COOK TIME: 1 HOUR (UNATTENDED), PLUS COOLING TIME

Rich Meat Sauce (page 164)

1 pound whole-milk, low-moisture mozzarella, coarsely shredded

One 15-ounce container whole-milk ricotta

½ cup finely grated Grana Padano or other good-quality Parmesan cheese

½ cup finely grated pecorino Romano

¼ cup chopped fresh parsley

1 teaspoon salt

½ teaspoon black pepper

1-pound package curly-edge lasagna noodles (regular noodles, not no-boil)

Additional grated Parmesan or Romano for passing, if you like

Note: If you choose to make this with cooked lasagna noodles or the very thin type of no-boil lasagna, there is no need to thin down the sauce.

1 Make the Rich Meat Sauce.

2 Make the cheese filling: Stir the mozzarella, ricotta, Parmesan, Romano, parsley, salt, and pepper together until well blended. The filling may be made up to a day in advance and refrigerated.

3 Assemble the lasagna: Stir 2 cups water into the sauce. Ladle 1 cup of the sauce over the bottom of a 13 x 9-inch lasagna pan. Cover the sauce with lasagna noodles, butting them up against each other or just slightly overlapping them. Cover the lasagna sheets with 2 cups of sauce. Remove about 1½ cups of the cheese filling and set aside. Crumble about half the remaining cheese mixture over the sauce. Repeat with another layer of noodles, 2 cups sauce, and cheese. Top with a layer of noodles, 1½ cups of sauce, and the reserved cheese filling. Cover with aluminum foil. The lasagna may be prepared up to a few hours in advance and refrigerated. There will be about 2 to 2½ cups of sauce left over. Scrape this sauce into a small saucepan and refrigerate until needed.

4 Heat the oven to 375°F. If refrigerated, remove the lasagna to room temperature while the oven heats.

5 Bake the lasagna 45 minutes. Remove the aluminum foil and bake until the center is very hot. (If you use an instant-read thermometer, the center of the lasagna should be between 170°F and 180°F.) Let stand 15 minutes before serving. Meanwhile, reheat the reserved sauce over low heat.

6 To serve, cut the lasagna into squares and plate. Pass the additional sauce and, if you like, grated cheese.

Sunday Gravy
(Slow-Simmered Tomato Sauce with Fennel Sausages, Meatballs, and Braciole, Served with Rigatoni)

SERVES 8 LUCKY PEOPLE

Is there a better example of food bringing people together than Sunday Gravy? Not in Sophia's world. Meaty-rich Italian sausages, homemade meatballs, and provolone-spinach-stuffed braciole, all simmered for hours in a slow-cooked tomato sauce. And, of course, the macaroni to go with it. (Before it was pasta, it was macaroni. And Sophia was cooking it!)

This is an undertaking, no mistake. It is also the ultimate do-ahead meal. Except for boiling the pasta, everything can be done in advance. Refrigerating the gravy overnight and reheating it slowly the day of only makes it better.

However, if you'd like to shave a little time off the prep, substitute 8 meaty (i.e., country-style) pork spare ribs for the braciole. Brown them in olive oil on the stovetop and add them to the gravy in place of the braciole, then keep going, adding the meatballs and sausages in their turn. Easier still, make the gravy with just the meatballs and sausages. It will still have the rich, browned-meat, slow-simmered flavor.

No matter what course you chart, start the meal with a double Antipasto Salad (page 153) and an Amaretto Sour (page 189).

Gravy Base

MAKES: ABOUT 16 CUPS • PREP TIME: 15 MINUTES • COOK TIME: 30 MINUTES UNTIL THE MEAT GOES IN

Three 28-ounce cans Italian plum tomatoes

3 tablespoons olive oil

2 medium yellow onions, diced (about 2 cups)

4 cloves garlic, chopped very fine

3 tablespoons tomato paste

¾ cup dry red wine

One 28-ounce can Italian tomato puree

1 Remove the cores and crush the tomatoes as described in step one of Rich Meat Sauce, page 164.

2 Heat the olive oil in a large (about 6-quart) pot over medium-low heat. Add the onion and garlic and cook, stirring, until the onions turn a light golden color and are tender, about 15 minutes. The onions should not sizzle. If they start browning around the edges, even a teeny bit, lower the heat.

3 When the onions are ready, stir in the tomato paste. Cook and stir until the onions are coated and the paste starts to stick, about 4 minutes. Pour in the red wine and let it boil, scraping the bottom of the pot, until it is very syrupy.

4 bay leaves

1 large pinch crushed red pepper flakes

Fine sea or kosher salt and freshly ground black pepper

4 Pour in the tomatoes and tomato puree. Add the bay leaves and red pepper. Bring to a boil. Season lightly with salt and pepper and adjust the heat so the gravy is at a gentle simmer.

5 Cook 30 to 45 minutes. If you haven't finished preparing and browning the braciole by then, just let the sauce simmer until the braciole are ready. At this point and throughout, check the gravy for thickness. If it is thicker than you'd like it, add water to thin it down a little.

Braciole (That's Brah-zhole to You!)

MAKES: 4 ROLLS • PREP TIME: 30 MINUTES • COOK TIME: 15 MINUTES TO BROWN; 1½ TO 2 HOURS IN THE GRAVY

FOR THE FILLING:
1 tablespoon olive oil

½ cup finely chopped yellow onion

1 large clove garlic, minced

One 5-ounce container baby spinach, washed and spun dry

½ cup plain bread crumbs

½ cup shredded sharp provolone

TO FILL AND BROWN THE BRACIOLE:
4 slices beef round, each no more than ½-inch thick and about 3 ounces (see note on page 170)

4 slices prosciutto, optional

Olive oil for browning

MAKE THE FILLING:

1 Heat the olive oil in a medium skillet over medium heat. Add the onion and garlic and cook, stirring, until the onion is softened and the garlic is fragrant, 6 to 8 minutes. Add a large handful of the spinach and cook until wilted down. Repeat with the remaining spinach. If there is any liquid on the bottom of the skillet, turn up the heat and cook it off.

2 Scrape the spinach mix into a bowl. Stir in the bread crumbs and provolone. Season with salt and pepper.

FILL AND BROWN THE BRACIOLE:

3 If they aren't already pounded, place one of the slices of beef round between two sheets of plastic wrap. Without walloping the beef, and with the smooth side of a meat mallet, pound the beef out to about ¼-inch thick. Start around the edges; that will make the center easier to do. Set aside and repeat with the remaining slices.

4 If you have enough room, lay out all the pounded beef slices. Top the center of each with a slice of prosciutto and some of the filling to run along the length of the prosciutto. Fold about ¾ inch of the sides of the beef over the filling, then fold the side closest to you up and over the filling. Roll up into a nice, snug roll. Tie in two places with kitchen twine or secure the edges with wooden picks to hold the roll together during browning and cooking.

5 Pour enough olive oil into a large heavy skillet to generously coat the bottom. Heat over medium heat until rippling. Add braciole to the pan and fry, turning as necessary, until well browned on all sides, about 10 minutes. If you used picks to secure the rolls, do your best to brown the beef around the picks. Slip the braciole into the gravy as they are done.

6 If you like, deglaze the pan. Pour the fat from the pan. Pour ½ cup or so of the wine you used to make the gravy or 2 ladles of the gravy into the pan. Bring to a boil and scrape up the brown bits from the pan. Scrape into the gravy.

Note: It is much easier to buy pre-pounded/tenderized slices of beef round from a butcher. If you are on friendly terms with yours, ask. When fully pounded, the slices of beef should measure 5 to 6 inches across.

Beef and Pork Meatballs

MAKES: 12 TO 14 LARGE MEATBALLS • PREP TIME: 15 MINUTES • COOK TIME: 15 MINUTES TO BROWN

1 pound ground beef

1 pound ground pork

2 eggs, beaten

⅓ cup plain bread crumbs

½ cup grated Parmesan cheese, preferably Grana Padano or Parmigiano-Reggiano

¼ cup grated Romano, preferably pecorino Romano

¼ cup chopped Italian parsley

1 small garlic clove, minced

¾ teaspoon fine sea or kosher salt

¼ teaspoon freshly ground black pepper

Olive oil, if browning on the stovetop

1 Crumble the ground beef and pork into a large bowl and pour the eggs over the meat. Scatter the bread crumbs, Parmesan and Romano cheeses, parsley, garlic, salt, and pepper over all. Work the mix with your hands (gloved or not—your call) until everything is evenly mixed.

2 Set a small baking sheet or large plate next to the meatball mix. Using about ¼ cup for each, roll the mix into balls and set them on the baking sheet.

Hard, messy way to brown: Pour enough olive oil into a large heavy skillet to generously coat the bottom. Heat over medium heat until rippling. Add as many meatballs as will fit without touching, and cook, turning as necessary, until well browned on all sides, about 8 minutes. Slip the meatballs into the gravy as they are done and replace them with new meatballs. When all the meatballs are browned, pour off the fat from the pan and scrape all the brown bits stuck to the pan into the gravy.

Easy, clean(er) way to brown: Heat the broiler to high. Line the meatballs up on a broiler pan and broil, turning once, until well browned on all sides, 8 to 10 minutes, depending on your broiler. Carefully slip the meatballs into the gravy.

The big question: Why would you choose the hard, messy way? To get to the part where you scrape all the wonderful browned stickies from the pan into the gravy.

3 Once the meatballs are all in the gravy, move on to the sausages.

───────────────── GOLDEN WISDOM ─────────────────

An easy way to tell when the mix is worked enough is to take a look at the parsley. When the little green flecks are evenly distributed, you're good to go.

Italian Sausage

If you're one of those prep whizzes who can handle two or three tasks at once, consider broiling the sausages while the meatballs are panfrying, or vice versa. Use the broiler here to give your stovetop a rest.

12 links (about 2½ pounds) sweet, hot, or a mix Italian pork sausages

Heat the broiler to low or medium with a rack about 6 inches from the broiler. Line the sausages up on a large broiler-proof pan and poke them all over with a wooden pick or fork. Broil the sausages until well browned. Remove the pan from the oven, flip the sausages, and brown the second side. Slip the sausages into the gravy.

───────────────── GOLDEN WISDOM ─────────────────

If cooking both hot and sweet sausages, slip a wooden pick about halfway into the ends of the hot sausages to tell them apart from the sweet ones. Remember to remove the picks before serving!

HERE'S A REVIEW SO FAR:

1 Make the gravy base.

2 While the gravy is coming to a boil, make the braciole filling.

3 Make, tie, and brown braciole; add them to the gravy base and cook for 1 hour before adding the other meats.

4 Make and brown the beef and pork meatballs; add them to the sauce when the time and gravy are ripe.

5 Cook the sausages and add them to the sauce.

Now that all the meats are in the gravy, simmer until the braciole is tender. That all depends on several factors, such as the meat you used for braciole and how long it took to get the meatballs and sausages together. Do remember at this and every other stage of gravy making to check the gravy and add water if it looks too thick.

If you are not cooking the gravy straight through, cool to room temperature. Pluck out the braciole, cut off the strings or pull out the picks, and return them to the pot. If you are cooking straight through, pluck the braciole out as soon as they are tender. Let stand until you can handle them, cut off the strings or pull out the picks, and return them to the gravy.

1½ pounds good-quality large macaroni shapes, such as rigatoni, penne, paccheri, or any other that tickles your pasta fancy

¾ cup grated Parmesan cheese, preferably Grana Padano or Parmigiano-Reggiano, or Romano cheese

¼ cup chopped Italian parsley, not necessary but nice, so chop a little extra when making the meatballs

PULLING IT ALL TOGETHER:

1 Reheat the gravy, if necessary, over very low heat, stirring gently occasionally (if not reheating, just let the gravy simmer).

2 Put a big pot of salted water on to boil; set up a large colander in the sink and a ladle and measuring cup near the stove. Stir the macaroni into the boiling water and cook, stirring occasionally, especially just after adding, until al dente (a minute or two less than package directions).

3 While the macaroni is boiling, remove the meats to a platter or bowl and cover to keep warm.

4 Ladle out about 1 cup of the cooking water and drain the macaroni; return the macaroni to the pot and place over low heat. Ladle enough gravy into the macaroni to coat it lightly; stir in about half the reserved cooking water and heat to simmering—the sauce should be smooth and shiny. If not, add a little more cooking water.

5 Stir in ¾ cup grated cheese and the parsley; check the seasoning and spoon into a big bowl. Serve the meats and macaroni, passing additional gravy and grated cheese on the side.

Enchiladas Rancheras

Sadly, Coco didn't last long on The Golden Girls, *but his memory lives on in the form of these delicious, cheesy, and simple-to-make enchiladas, fancy enough for a dinner party. Prepare the sauce and filling up to 2 days in advance. Soften the tortillas, fill them, and arrange them in the baking dish up to 3 hours in advance.*

MAKES: 4 SERVINGS • PREP TIME: AROUND 50 MINUTES • COOK TIME: 55 MINUTES

FOR THE SAUCE:

1 tablespoon vegetable oil

1 cup finely chopped onion

½ cup chopped red bell pepper

½ small jalapeño, cored, seeded, and finely chopped

1 large garlic clove, minced

¾ teaspoon ground cumin

¼ teaspoon ground coriander

One 14-ounce can roasted diced tomatoes

½ cup Rotisserie Chicken Broth (page 71) or store-bought reduced-sodium chicken broth

¼ cup chopped fresh cilantro

MAKE THE SAUCE:

1 Heat 1 tablespoon vegetable oil in a 2-quart saucepan over medium heat. Stir in the onion, red bell peppers, jalapeño, garlic, cumin, and coriander. Cook, stirring often, until the vegetables are softened but not browned, about 10 minutes.

2 Stir in the tomatoes and their liquid and the chicken broth. Heat to boiling, then adjust the heat so the sauce is simmering. Simmer until the sauce is lightly thickened, about 30 minutes. Stir in the cilantro. The sauce can be used immediately or held at room temperature for up to a few hours, or covered and refrigerated for up to 4 days. If not used immediately, reheat over low heat until bubbling.

MAKE THE ENCHILADAS:

3 Heat the broiler to high, with a rack positioned about 4 inches from the broiler. Leave any stalk on the bottom of the corn that sticks out past the end of the cob in place. Rub the corn very lightly with vegetable oil and put on a broiler pan. Broil, turning a few times, until the kernels are very dark—a few burnt kernels are okay—on all sides, about 12 minutes. Let stand at room temperature until cool enough to handle. Stand up one ear at a time, holding it by the stalk and resting the tip on a cutting board. Use a small knife to shave off all the cooked kernels. Set ½ cup aside and put the rest in a medium bowl. Change the oven to bake, and heat to 375°F.

4 Chop the chicken until the pieces are about the same size as the corn kernels. Add to the corn in the bowl. Add 1½ cups of the grated cheese and the peas, and stir well. Taste and add salt if needed.

FOR THE ENCHILADAS:
2 ears corn, shucked, silk removed

Vegetable oil

1½ cups diced meat from a rotisserie chicken

6 ounces shredded jack cheese (about 2½ cups)

½ cup frozen peas, defrosted

Fine sea salt, if needed

8 corn tortillas

Mexican crema (see note)

5 Lightly spray an 11 x 9-inch baking pan with nonstick cooking spray. Add enough of the vegetable oil to a small (about 6-inch) skillet to coat the bottom. Heat over medium heat until the oil is ripping. Carefully lay out one of the tortillas in the pan. Cook, turning once, until the tortilla begins to blister and bubble around the edges. Flip and cook about 10 seconds. Lift onto a small plate. Repeat with the remaining tortillas, adding a little oil as necessary and stacking them atop the first tortillas to keep them warm and soft.

6 Lay one of the tortillas out on a cutting board. Spoon about ⅓ cup of the filling in a line down the center of the tortilla. Fold one end of the tortilla over the filling and roll up into a tight roll. Lay flap-down in the prepared baking dish. Repeat with the remaining filling and tortillas.

7 Sprinkle the remaining cheese (about 1 cup) evenly over the enchiladas in the dish. Cover with aluminum foil. The enchiladas can be prepared up to 2 hours in advance. Refrigerate in the dish and bring to room temperature about 30 minutes before cooking.

8 Bake the enchiladas 20 minutes. Remove the foil and bake until the cheese is lightly browned around the edges, 5 to 10 minutes. Let rest 5 minutes before serving.

BRING IT ALL TOGETHER:

9 Lift 2 enchiladas onto a plate and spoon a thick ribbon of sauce over their center. Scatter some of the reserved corn kernels over and around the enchiladas. Drizzle the plate with crema and serve.

Note: Mexican crema is available in all Latin groceries or the Latin section of bigger supermarkets. It is thin, of drizzling consistency, and mildly tangy. If you cannot find it, spoon about ½ cup of sour cream into a bowl and slowly add cold water, stirring, until the sour cream is drizzle-able.

TO CRISP OR NOT TO CRISP? ———————————

Coco liked the filling wrapped in a crisp corn tortilla, so he baked the enchiladas naked (Blanche approved). The sauce is added just before serving along with a smattering of sweet-savory kernels of roasted corn. If you prefer a more traditional dish—enchiladas topped with sauce and cheese before baking—follow this simple change: Line up the filled tortillas as described in the recipe. Spoon the room-temperature sauce over the enchiladas to cover them completely. Sprinkle the reserved cheese over the sauce, cover, and bake as described in the recipe. The tortillas and cheese will not crisp up as they do in the naked version. To serve, lift two sauce-and-cheese-covered enchiladas onto a plate. Scatter some of the reserved roasted corn kernels over the enchiladas, and drizzle the enchiladas and plate with crema.

Escarole and White Beans

This is a meal unto itself or, in its "medium" version, paired with ziti or other chunky pasta like rigatoni. When Sophia makes the soupy version, it's always topped with pecorino Romano cheese. Leave the anchovies out if you don't like them or if you'd like to make this a vegetarian dish.

MAKES: 4 SERVINGS • PREP TIME: 15 MINUTES • COOK TIME: 12 TO 20 MINUTES

2 medium heads (about 1½ pounds) escarole

2 tablespoons olive oil

6 cloves garlic (or fewer, if you like)

2 anchovy fillets (if you shuddered when you read this, leave them out)

A healthy pinch or two of crushed red pepper

1½ cups cooked white beans, with liquid or one 15-ounce can white beans (if using canned, drain and rinse them)

½ cup vegetable or chicken stock

A piece of pecorino or Parmesan cheese

1 Prep the escarole: Pull off any dark, wilted, or yellowing leaves. Cut the head in half through the core, then cut out the core. Cut the halves into 1-inch (or so) squares. Wash them (see sidebar) and spin them dry in a salad spinner. There will be about 12 lightly packed cups. It sounds like a lot, but as with all leafy greens, they will shrink radically when you cook them.

2 Heat the olive oil in a large deep skillet over medium heat. While that's heating up, slice the garlic thinly. Add the garlic to the oil along with the anchovies, if you're using them, and the crushed red pepper. Shake the pan until the garlic starts to brown around the edges and the anchovies "melt," about 3 minutes.

3 Stir about half the escarole into the skillet, season it very lightly, and stir until it wilts enough to add the rest of the escarole. Stir the second batch, season lightly with salt, and cook until it is wilted. Stir in the beans and broth. Heat to boiling.

4 You have a choice: cook for just a few minutes for escarole with more bite and a soupier sauce, or cook until the escarole is tender and the broth is almost completely gone—or anywhere in between. (Don't ask Sophia which version is best. She'll just say, "That's like asking me who is my favorite child. Oh, wait, it's Gloria.") Choose the halfway cooked version for saucing pasta (see opposite). Pull the skillet off the heat. Serve the escarole and beans hot, let it stand at room temperature for up to a few hours, or refrigerate for up to 3 days.

5 Reheat the escarole and beans over low heat, check the seasonings, and serve in a warm bowl, passing grated cheese at the table. Or pass a block of cheese and a vegetable peeler and let people shave their own cheese over their bowls.

Variation: Pasta with Escarole and Beans

MAKES: 3 TO 4 SERVINGS

Prepare the escarole and beans as described above. Just before starting, set a large pot of salted water over high heat to boil. Simmer the escarole and beans until about half the liquid is cooked off, and remove the pan from the heat. When the water comes to a boil, stir about half a 1-pound box of ziti, rigatoni, or shells into the pot. Cook, stirring often (especially during the first couple of minutes), until the pasta is al dente. Ladle off and reserve about 1 cup of the pasta cooking water. Drain the pasta and return to the pot. Add as much of the escarole and beans to the pot as you like and enough of the pasta cooking liquid to make a medium-consistency sauce. It's okay if this pasta is borderline soupy, if that's what you like. Bring to a boil, ladle into warm bowls, and festoon with the cheese of your choice.

WASHING GREENS

The easiest way to wash a large amount of greens is in your kitchen sink. Clean the sink with soap and water, and rinse it thoroughly. While you are prepping the greens, run cool water to fill the sink about halfway. Put the prepped greens into the sinkful of water and swish them around a bit. Let them sit for a minute or so to give the dirt and grit a chance to settle to the bottom. Swish and let stand again. With your hands, lift the greens to a large colander to drain. If the greens still feel gritty or if there is a lot of dirt and grit that has settled to the bottom of the sink, drain the water, rinse the sink, and repeat the washing. Spin the clean greens dry in batches. This works for all kinds of greens; greens cleaned and spun dry this way last up to 2 days if you roll them up loosely in several sheets of paper towels and slide them into a plastic bag. Don't seal or tie up the plastic bag.

Stovetop Vegetable Casserole

Like her Sicilian counterparts, Sophia knows the appeal of the deep flavors of slow-cooked vegetables. The colors may not be the brightest, but the depth of flavor more than makes up for that.

MAKES: 4 SERVINGS • PREP TIME: 15 MINUTES • COOK TIME: 20 MINUTES

½ pound string beans, ends trimmed

½ small head cauliflower (about 1 pound), cut into 1-inch (or so) florets

½ large or 1 small red or yellow onion, thinly sliced

Sea salt

2 tablespoons olive oil

2 cloves garlic, thinly sliced

Freshly ground black pepper

1 Place the string beans, cauliflower, and onion in a large—about 10-inch—deep skillet and pour in ¼ cup water. Season lightly with salt. Bring to a boil over medium heat, cover the skillet, and cook 5 minutes.

2 Uncover the skillet and cook until the bottom of the skillet is dry, about 5 minutes.

3 Pour in the olive oil, add the garlic, and cook, stirring occasionally and gently, to avoid breaking up the florets, until the vegetables are very tender but not falling apart, about 8 minutes. (Because the vegetables have been steamed, they won't brown.) Season to taste with salt and pepper and serve hot or at room temperature.

IMPROVVISANDO

If you have broccoli in the crisper, substitute for the cauliflower. Likewise with brussels sprouts or mushrooms. Any member of the onion family, such as shallots, leeks (white parts), or Vidalia onions, can be substituted for the red or yellow onion.

Gorgonzola Mushrooms

While she's prepping these, Sophia trims up the stems and cooks them with the rest of the mushrooms. When they're done, she nibbles on them with a nip of sherry. If Gorgonzola isn't your thing, simply prepare the mushrooms without.

MAKES: 4 SERVINGS • PREP TIME: 5 MINUTES • COOK TIME: 10 MINUTES, PLUS 5 MINUTES RESTING TIME

One 10-ounce container firm mushrooms, such as cremini or white button

8 ounces shiitake mushrooms (or a second container of firm mushrooms)

3 tablespoons olive oil

2 tablespoons fresh lemon juice

½ teaspoon kosher salt

Freshly ground black pepper

⅔ cup crumbled Gorgonzola cheese (about 2 ounces)

2 tablespoons chopped fresh parsley

1 Preheat the broiler to high with the rack about 4 inches from the heat.

2 Snap off the stems of the cremini or button mushrooms. (Trim the stems and cook them along with the caps if you like.) Cut off and discard the shiitake stems. Wipe the mushroom caps clean with a damp paper towel or the palm of your hand and place them in a large bowl. Slowly pour 2 tablespoons of the olive oil over them while tossing. Add the lemon juice, salt, and pepper to taste. Toss to mix. Let stand, tossing two or three times, 5 minutes.

3 Arrange the mushrooms cap side down on a metal broiler pan (a 12 x 9-inch quarter sheet works beautifully). The mushroom caps will overlap; they shrink as they cook. Broil until they begin to brown, about 6 minutes. Turn the mushrooms, sprinkle the Gorgonzola over them, and continue broiling until the caps are lightly browned and tender when poked with the tip of a knife and the cheese is bubbly, about 4 minutes.

4 Transfer the mushrooms to a platter, leaving the juices behind. Add the remaining 1 tablespoon of olive oil and the parsley to the juice. Stir well and spoon over the mushrooms. Serve warm or at room temperature.

GOLDEN WISDOM

Many mushrooms come in a 10-ounce plastic container. To clean the mushrooms easily, empty them out onto the counter, rinse out the container, and wipe it dry with a paper towel. You now have a damp paper towel to wipe the mushrooms clean and a place to put them after you do.

Golden Cauliflower Trees

MAKES: ABOUT 20 TREES • PREP TIME: 30 MINUTES • COOK TIME: 5 MINUTES

1 small head cauliflower, about 2½ pounds

Fine salt and freshly ground black pepper

½ cup fine plain bread crumbs

3 tablespoons finely grated pecorino or Parmesan cheese

3 tablespoons chopped Italian parsley

⅛ teaspoon garlic powder, optional

½ cup all-purpose flour

2 eggs beaten with 1 tablespoon water

Vegetable oil

Notes: To test the oil, hold a tree with a pair of tongs and dip a corner of the tree into the oil. When it gives off a lively sizzle, the oil is ready.

During frying, adjust the heat so the cauliflower gives off a lively sizzle without spattering, not so hot the edges burn and not so cool that they sit there doing nothing.

To give you a little distance from the sizzling oil, use a slotted spoon or small pair of tongs to gently lay the trees in the oil and turn them.

Carefully lay as many trees in the oil as will fit without touching—the oil should be sizzling between the trees.

1 To get the distinctive tree shape: Trim the bottom of the cauliflower stem even with the cauliflower and remove all the green leaves from the base. Set the cauliflower flat side down and cut in half through the stem. Set one half of the cauliflower aside for another dish (see Stovetop Vegetable Casserole, page 178). Turn the other half cut side down on the cutting board. Cut crosswise into ¾-inch slices. This is important—the slices should be thick enough to hold together but thin enough to cook through. If some of the cauliflower crumbles, add the crumbles to the reserved cauliflower. Separate the cauliflower into "trees," handling them gently. Some trees will be larger than others. None, however, will be as large as the old oak tree on Freida Claxton's property.

2 Steam the trees over boiling water until a paring knife meets just a little resistance going through the stem, about 5 minutes. Carefully remove trees to a baking sheet lined with paper towels. Sprinkle the trees with salt and pepper while they are still warm. Cool them to room temperature.

3 Meanwhile, mix together the bread crumbs, grated cheese, parsley, and garlic powder, if using. Dredge the trees, two or three at a time, in flour, gently shaking off excess flour before adding them to the egg. Roll them in the egg to coat completely, hold them over the bowl until all the excess egg has dripped back into the bowl, and then lay them in the seasoned bread crumbs. Coat them evenly, patting the crumbs on to help them stick. Put the cauliflower on a wire rack to dry while you coat the remaining trees.

4 Heat ½ inch of vegetable oil in a large heavy pan over medium heat. Cook, turning once carefully, until the trees are golden brown on both sides, about 2 minutes per side (see notes).

5 Drain the trees on a paper towel and serve hot, warm, or at room temperature.

Carrot Cake Goes to Miami

A girl can't live in Miami forever without soaking up a little of the tropical vibe. Sophia's beloved carrot cake has evolved over the years into this golden beauty, rich with carrots, orange flavor, and mangos. If you have friends with nut issues, simply leave the toasted coconut and pecans off the top of the cake—there are no nuts in the cake itself, so everyone can enjoy!

MAKES: 12 SERVINGS • PREP TIME: 45 MINUTES TOTAL • BAKE TIME: 25 MINUTES

FOR THE CAKE:

2¼ cups all-purpose flour, plus more for flouring the cake pans

1 teaspoon baking soda

1 teaspoon baking powder

½ teaspoon fine sea or kosher salt

½ teaspoon ground cinnamon

⅛ teaspoon each ground cloves and ground allspice

1 cup vegetable oil, plus more for greasing the cake pans

¾ cup granulated sugar

¾ cup lightly packed brown sugar

4 large eggs

¼ cup freshly squeezed or bottled orange juice

1 teaspoon vanilla extract

Grated zest of 1 large orange

2½ cups coarsely shredded carrots (about 5 medium carrots)

½ cup diced dried mango (see notes)

MAKE THE CAKE:

1 Heat the oven to 350°F with a rack in the center position. Oil and flour two 9-inch round cake pans and set them aside.

2 Sift together the flour, baking soda, baking powder, salt, cinnamon, cloves, and allspice. Set aside.

3 In a large bowl using a hand mixer or in the bowl of a stand mixer, beat together the oil, granulated sugar, and brown sugar until foamy and evenly blended. Beat in the eggs, one at a time, scraping the bottom and sides of the bowl once or twice. Beat in the orange juice, vanilla, and orange zest. Switch to a rubber spatula and stir in the carrots and mango. Fold the flour mixture into the batter, scraping the sides and bottom of the bowl as you do, just until no streaks of flour remain. Don't overmix.

4 Divide the batter between the prepared pans. Bake until deep golden brown and a cake tester or wooden pick comes out clean, about 25 minutes. Cool 20 minutes, then remove the cakes by inverting them onto a cooling rack and cool completely.

FOR THE CREAM CHEESE FROSTING:

16 ounces cream cheese, at room temperature

¾ cups confectioners' sugar

2 tablespoons orange juice

Large pinch salt

½ cup toasted pecan halves or toasted chopped walnuts

¼ cup toasted unsweetened flaked coconut

MAKE THE FROSTING AND FINISH THE CAKE:

5 While the cakes are cooling, beat the cream cheese, confectioners' sugar, orange juice, and salt together until smooth and fluffy.

6 Put one cake layer on a plate or cake plate bottom side up. Spread half the frosting over the layer, pushing it right up to edge of the cake and making an even layer. Place the other cake layer, bottom side up, over the first and press very gently so a little of the frosting can be seen from the sides of the cake. Frost the top layer with the rest of the filling, again making an even layer and going right up to the edges of the cake. (Don't frost the sides.) Decorate the top of the cake with toasted coconut and pecan halves if you like.

Notes: Dried mango is available sweetened and unsweetened. Sweetened is easier to cut and, well, sweeter. Unsweetened is more intensely flavored and less sweet. It's your pick. But if you do choose unsweetened, pour a little boiling water over the whole pieces in a heatproof bowl and let stand 15 minutes. Drain and cool before dicing. This will make them easier to cut and give them a softer texture in the finished cake.

The components of the cake can be made up to a day in advance. Keep the cake layers and coconut and pecans, if using, at room temperature. Refrigerate the frosting, but bring it to room temperature about 2 hours before using.

Old-School Banana-Poppy Seed Cake with Banana Glaze

Back in the day, Sophia knew just about every Italian banana guy in Brooklyn—and that's saying something! They used to leave spotty brown bananas, the perfect type for this cake, on her stoop. She returned the favor with a nice big slice of this moist and rich cake the next time they drove down the block.

MAKES: ONE 9-INCH CAKE/12 SERVINGS • PREP TIME: 20 MINUTES • BAKE TIME: 50 MINUTES

FOR THE CAKE:

1 cup mashed banana (from about 2 good-size spotty bananas)

1 lemon

2 cups all-purpose flour or white whole-wheat flour

2 teaspoons baking powder

¼ teaspoon salt

1 tablespoon plus 1 teaspoon (aka 4 teaspoons) poppy seeds, plus more for sprinkling over finished cake

1½ sticks butter, at room temperature, plus more for the pan

½ cup light brown sugar

½ cup granulated sugar

2 eggs, at room temperature

1½ teaspoons vanilla extract

MAKE THE CAKE:

1 Heat the oven to 350°F. Grease a 9-inch cake pan with butter and coat lightly with flour.

2 Mash enough banana to measure 1 cup. (Save any leftover banana for the glaze.) Zest the lemon and stir into the banana mash along with the juice from half the lemon. Sift the flour, baking powder, and salt together into a bowl. Stir in 4 teaspoons of poppy seeds and set the bowl aside.

3 In the bowl of a stand mixer or in a bowl using a handheld mixer, beat the butter and sugars together until fluffy and very pale, about 4 minutes. Stop a few times to scrape the bottom and sides of the bowl. Beat in the eggs one at a time, scraping the bowl after each. Beat in the banana-lemon mixture and vanilla extract. Scrape the bowl again. Don't be surprised if the batter looks a little curdled at this point.

4 With the mixer on low speed, mix in about ⅓ of the flour mixture just until blended. Add half the milk and blend. Continue adding the milk and flour mix, using half the remaining flour, the remaining milk, and then all the remaining flour. Scrape the bowl well and blend by hand until the batter is evenly mixed.

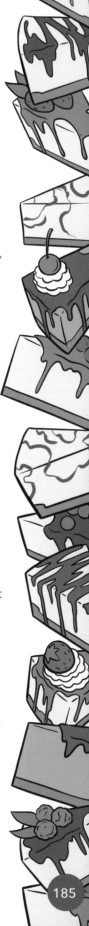

1 cup milk

FOR THE GLAZE:
½ cup mashed banana

Juice of half a lemon

6 ounces cream cheese

¼ cup confectioners' sugar

½ teaspoon vanilla

5 Scrape the batter into the prepared pan. Bake until golden brown on top and a wooden pick inserted into the center of the cake comes out clean, about 50 minutes.

6 Cool on a wire rack for 20 minutes. Flip out of the pan onto the rack, bottom side up. Cool completely.

MAKE THE GLAZE AND FINISH:

7 Mash enough banana to measure ½ cup. Squeeze the juice from the other half of the lemon into the banana. For a super-smooth glaze, process the cream cheese, confectioners' sugar, and vanilla in a food processor until well blended. Add the banana-lemon mixture and process until very smooth. If you don't mind a few lumps, beat the cream cheese and confectioners' sugar in a medium bowl until smooth, then beat in the banana-lemon mixture and vanilla.

8 When the cake is completely cool, set the cake on the rack over a sheet of parchment paper or plastic wrap. Scrape the glaze onto the center of the cake. Use an offset spatula or large spoon to nudge the glaze toward the edge of the cake, covering the top and letting some of the glaze drip artfully down the sides. Sprinkle some poppy seeds over the glaze. If you can wait, let the glazed cake set for an hour or two; the glaze will be firmer and the cake easier to slice. Once the glaze is set, move the cake to a serving plate. Serve at room temperature or chilled. The cake will keep up to 2 days wrapped with plastic wrap.

My mother always used to say, "The older you get, the better you get, unless you're a banana."

BANANA CUPCAKES

The batter can be turned into cupcakes, with or without the glaze (makes 10 large or 16 medium). Reduce baking time to about 35 minutes.

Amaretto Sour

Fruity, nutty, and not too sweet, no wonder this is Sophia's favorite drink!

MAKES: 2 COCKTAILS • PREP TIME: 5 MINUTES

1 orange

1 jar maraschino cherries

4 to 5 amaretti (small, often paper-wrapped almond-flavored cookies), optional

½ cup amaretto

1 tablespoon freshly squeezed lemon juice

Ice cubes

1 Cut the orange into chunks (regular-size wedges cut crosswise), using one per drink plus a few extras. Pick out the seeds, if any. Remove one cherry per drink from the jar to a double thickness of paper towels to drain. Use thin skewers or wooden picks to spear one cherry and one orange chunk. Line up the fruit skewers on a small plate.

2 Put the amaretti, if using, in a heavy sealable plastic bag. Roll over them with a rolling pin or bottle until finely crushed. Empty the crumbs onto a small plate. Rub the rims of 2 rocks glasses with an orange chunk and dunk the rims in the crumbs to make an even, fine coating of crumbs. Set the glasses aside. This can be done hours in advance.

3 Combine the amaretto, lemon juice, and ½ to 1 teaspoon of the liquid from the maraschino cherries in a cocktail shaker. Add 4 to 6 ice cubes and put the lid on firmly. Shake very well and pour into the glasses, dividing the ice cubes. Garnish each with a fruit skewer.

Citrus-Almond Biscotti

MAKES: ABOUT 30 BISCOTTI • PREP TIME: 1 HOUR • BAKE TIME: 1 HOUR 5 MINUTES

1¼ cups slivered almonds

2¾ cups all-purpose flour

1½ teaspoons baking powder

½ teaspoon salt

¼ cup olive oil

3 tablespoons unsalted butter, softened

¾ cup granulated sugar

3 large eggs, at room temperature

3 tablespoons lemon juice

1 tablespoon pure orange extract

2 teaspoons finely grated lemon zest

1 Heat the oven to 350°F with a rack in the center position. Spread the almonds out in a single layer on a baking sheet and toast, stirring once, until light golden brown, 10 to 11 minutes. Remove and cool but leave the oven on. Line a large baking sheet with parchment paper or a silicone baking mat.

2 Sift the flour, baking powder, and salt onto a sheet of parchment paper or into a bowl.

3 Beat the olive oil and butter together with a handheld mixer until smooth. Gradually add the sugar while blending. Scrape the sides and bottom of the bowl, then beat in the eggs, one at a time, stopping after each to scrape the bottom and sides of the bowl. Beat in the lemon juice, orange extract, and lemon zest. Stir in the dry ingredients and almonds.

4 Divide the dough in half and place the halves on the prepared baking sheet. Using a spoon, shape each into a 2- to 2½-inch-wide by 1½-inch-high log. Don't worry if they're not perfectly even. Different-size logs will produce different-size biscotti.

5 Bake until the top is cracked and firm when pressed lightly, about 25 minutes. Remove and cool 30 minutes. Reduce the oven temp to 300°F.

6 Gently saw the loaves into ½-inch slices with a serrated knife. Turn the slices on their sides. Bake, turning once, until very lightly browned around the edges, about 40 minutes. Leave the biscotti in the oven and turn the oven off.

7 Remove the biscotti after 30 minutes and cool them on a rack completely before storing in an airtight container. The biscotti will be better the day after baking and will keep for up to 4 days at room temperature.